The Wallaby Trade

Rob Booker

Counter-Trend Trading for Stocks, Futures, & Forex

Also by Rob Booker

Books:
"Adventures of a Currency Trader"
"The Currency Trader's Handbook"

eBooks:
"Forex Strategy 10: Low Risk/High Return Currency Trading"

To all the Wallabies who follow me on Twitter, this is for you.
Thanks for reading all the crap I've been writing.

Contents

FREE STUFF

The Wallaby Indicator is free and available here:
http://www.WallabyTrade.com

You can follow Wallaby trades on Twitter at:
http://www.twitter.com/wallabytrade

INTRODUCTION
WHAT YOU GET WITH THIS BOOK

I'm going to share every last detail about my favorite method of short-term trading. And you can apply this method to longer-term trading, too. This book is filled with charts, step by step instructions, some stories, and quite a bit of offensive language. It shouldn't take you long to read the book, but I hope you come back to it again and again as you learn to trade the system.

I've had the Wallaby indicator built for a number of charting platforms, and as mentioned a few pages ago, you can have the indicator for free. In fact, as you'll learn in chatper 1, you can even trade the method without the indicator.

Most of all, I look forward to hearing from you. Please contact me on Twitter (preferred) or Facebook. This isn't your average trading book. But after all, you're not the average trader. And I want to hear what you do with what you've learned.

Let's dive in. And be warned: It does get a bit sticky at times.

1

Chapter One

What the hell is a Wallaby?

A few years ago, I was in Australia doing a seminar. During these seminars I traded live. I showed hundreds of charts and broke down every system I used into specific steps. It was the most exhausting work I've ever done. I met some of my best trading friends at these events — people I'm still in touch with to this day.

I generally invented something new to share with each seminar group. Creating new systems was fun. I'd have something fresh and exciting to offer the traders. They knew they were getting the very best I had to give, as well as the latest information. I had more fun. They had more fun. When we had more fun, we made more money. You get the point.

Well, at this Australia seminar I introduced the Wallaby Indicator, which I built in the lobby of the hotel. I can't remember the name of the hotel chain, but the beds were crap. It felt like you were lying on Styrofoam. Nevertheless, the view of Darling Harbour from my room was awesome, and I spent a lot of time standing in front of the window, wondering what the hell time it was, and wondering why I continued to fly around the world.[1]

---

1. I am not making this up: When I flew on this trip from San Francisco to Sydney, the gate agent realized that the name on my passport did not match my airline ticket. This was because some jackhole at the U.S. Passport office could not spell, and because I had been too lazy to take the time to send it in for corrections. Because the gate agent was a little bit flirty, and because I was willing to act a little bit gay, I got on the plane, anyway, and he even upgraded me to First Class. Fancy!

Here is a picture I took from my hotel window:

FIG. 1-1: The view from my room in Sydney, Australia.

While sitting in the lobby of the Novotel (wow! I remembered the hotel name — see, I haven't damaged every last brain cell in my skull by flying millions of miles) for a few days, trying to force my body into submission to a 14-hour time change, it occurred to me that I'd like to see a bunch of Stochastic Oscillators on top of one another.

No, this wasn't some kind of kinky dream I'd had (for that, see Chapter 2), but rather, it was a sincere desire to see what would happen if I started overlapping indicators. Would these indicators get along? Would they mate? What would they produce?

Okay, maybe it did get a little bit kinky. I get that way about trading.

Anyway, the next thing you know, I'm staying up late and waking up early, and I'm furiously typing away on my laptop, programming a new indicator. I took standard indicators and used them to do new things. Time passed without me even noticing. I skipped meals — even the yummy breakfast potatoes from the Novotel, which were served up by this really cute Czech girl.

After a couple of days, the indicator was complete. I was in Australia, so I called it the Wallaby.

And now you ask again: What the hell is a Wallaby?

Well, I'm glad you asked.

The Wallaby Is an Indicator
Built From the Stochastic Oscillator.

An oscillator is something (duh!) that "oscillates," or swings back and forth. When you place an oscillator on your chart, you're attempting to get a feel for the swinging movement, back and forth, that a financial instrument makes.

At the time I built the Wallaby, I'd already been using oscillators in my everyday trading. You probably have, as well. From the Relative Strength Index ("RSI") to the

Commodity Channel Index ("CCI") to the Stochastic, there are probably hundreds of oscillators out there. And they are meant to do just one thing, really: They tell you when a financial instrument is overbought or oversold.

For the purposes of this book, I'll use the letters "OB" to refer to overbought and "OS" to refer to oversold, and I'll use these interchangeably, just to shake things up. By the way, I'll also use the words stock, currency pair, futures contract, security and financial instrument — all to refer to the types of things you can trade with the Wallaby.

A financial instrument is said to be overbought when it's gone up so high that people/charts/astrologists think it's coming back down again. Most oscillators have a set of lines that will show that this overbought exists. This is hard to describe with just words, so I thought I'd write a poem about it:

> *There once was a stock named Ford*
> *It never moved, so people got bored*
> *It went overbought*
> *And I bought the stock*
> *And I can't rhyme, so the end of this limerick*
> *makes no sense.*

All right, it's clear that the poem idea failed. You can be sure that I will try it again later on, to see if I can make it any worse.

Instead of trying to work with a poem, let's just move onward and show you what an oscillator looks like when you plot it on a chart. Behold:

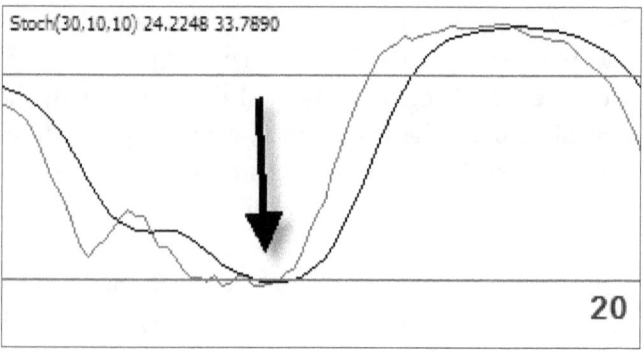

FIG. 1-2: Oversold!

And also:

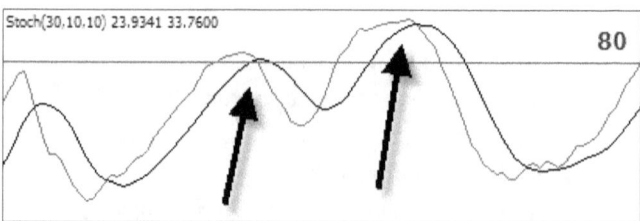

FIG. 1-3: Overbought!

That's the regular Stochastic Oscillator. The indicator will show two lines, one line that moves faster than the other. When the faster line goes above 80, we call that overbought, and when the faster line goes below 20, we call that oversold. When both lines go above 80 or below 20, we get our britches on and get ready to trade.

The Stochastic Oscillator was invented in 1492 by Theodore Roosevelt.[2] It's premised on the belief that as a financial instrument travels higher, the momentum with which it travels will slow down. Imagine for a moment that you're running uphill. You are probably able to go faster at the bottom of the hill than at the top. It's the same idea with an overbought reading on the Stochastic Oscillator. Remember, an oscillator measures the ability of something to swing back and forth — and when it swings upward (overbought), it's going to eventually swing back lower.

But the Stochastic doesn't just measure overbought conditions, right? It's also used to predict when a price may have moved down so far that it should not be able to travel any lower. That's a pretty wild statement to make, since exactly predicting price movement is actually impossible.

Anyway, that's oversold: The price of a stock has traveled so far low that we think it's ready for a swing back upward. As a financial instrument travels lower, it's eventually

---

2. This is not actually true. It was invented by George Lane, one of the most famous technical analysts of all time. He goes way back — he started his career at E.F. Hutton (so you know when he talked, people listened) in 1950.

going to get tired, and the momentum will slow down. Price will move a bit lower. It even might create a giant spike downward in one last swan dive. All of this pushes our Stochastic lines below the 20 mark. That's a sign that a stock has gone oversold, and it's an early warning sign that it could be ready to head higher.

Here's the formula for the oscillator (H = high, L = low):

$$100 \, \frac{CLOSE(i) - L(n)}{H(n) - L(n)}$$

If that formula seems confusing, you're not alone. In the 50 years since the Stochastic was invented, not one person has ever gone through the trouble to calculate it by hand, or even using a calculator. It's not necessary. The charts do all the hard work for you. All that formula means is that the Stochastic compares the closing price of a financial instrument to its recent price range. Your charts will automatically do all this math for you, so we don't need to have a big, long conversation about it. As long as you plug in some numbers to start it off, the charts can do the rest.

The numbers you need to plug in are for the number of bars you're going to look back over in order to get your high to low range, and then a number for the moving average associated with the "%D" part of the formula. You have complete control over these numbers. You are the master of the Stochastic. The Big Cheese. The one who calls the shots. You get the idea.

Most people choose 7, 3, 3, for their settings on the Stochastic. It's used by 99% of all the people in the world who ever plot this indicator. Only Kim Jong-il of North Korea and Rob Booker use different settings. To keep things simple, we'll stick with the 7,3,3 settings right now.

Once you set it up on your charts, here's what it looks like:

FIG. 1-4: A chart with the Stochastic Oscillator

The Problem

What? A problem?! Already?

The problem with just plotting the indicator "as is" comes when you try to build a complete trading system out of showing the standard oscillator. Of course you can plot it on your charts and buy when the oscillator goes below 20, or sell when it goes above 80. Or you can do something slightly more original — and do the opposite of what I just said — buying when it goes above 80 and selling when it goes below 20. Millions of traders have come and gone and done exactly those things.

While that might be enough for some traders, it's not enough for me. And I'm guessing you bought this book because it's not enough for you, either. Just putting some colorful lines on my charts isn't going to be enough to create a trading method. I don't want to look at the same thing, in the same way, as most other traders. I'm a counter-trend trader by choice, and I'm a counter-trend person in my life. If I find out that everyone is watching the same movie, I cross it off my list. If I find out that everyone is plotting the same indicator in the same way, I look for a way to do it differently. The last thing I want to do is follow the majority of traders. Especially because the majority of traders lose money.

What I'm Trying to Say

People all around the world pick up a book and learn something and follow it blindly. God, I'm happy that's not the way you're approaching this book. I want you to think critically, talk to me on Twitter, talk to the Wallaby on Facebook, and generally pick this all apart and put it back together again. I'm going to guide you through that process, teach you how to think about the Wallaby and show you lots of examples — and then you're going to have a system that you can call your own.

As for the rest of the people in the world that don't think critically about trading systems, well, good for them. I would gladly sit a shouting monkey in front of a computer and have it trade against those people, and I bet you the monkey would win. Hell, on some days the monkey would beat me.

FIG. 1-5:
"Bobo the Trading Monkey"
after a loss.

After the monkey finished beating himself up for making common beginners' mistakes, he'd probably have a banana. And after the banana, he'd probably throw some poo around until he got tired. And after that, when he had exhausted all his other diversions, the monkey would probably ask himself, "Why don't I mix this up a bit and show the indicator in a different way?" Then, off to the bathroom with our little primate friend, where he'd wash his hands and come back to the computer and get to work.[3]

That's pretty much what I did, too. I didn't fling any poo around, but I did wash up and get back to work — and thought about displaying a common indicator (the Stochastic) in a unique way.

I decided to show the Stochastic overlapping on top of another Stochastic, overlapping on top of yet another. It sounds crazy. It is, I admit, just a little bit insane. It was like a three-layer Mexican dip, only slightly less spicy.

Here's what I did:

> I put the 1-minute Stochastic 7,3,3, on the chart. *(cheese layer)*
> I then put the 5-minute Stochastic on top of it. *(second cheese layer!)*
> I then put the 15-minute Stochastic on top of that. *(third cheese layer!)*

And what I ended up with was three oscillators, from three different time-frame charts, all on the same chart.

First let's take a look at what it looks like when you do that, and then I'll explain why I used the time-frame charts that I did.

FIG. 1-6: The Wallaby

3. I strongly suggest that any time you see an indicator — no matter what it is, including the one you're reading about in this book — that you immediately look to change the settings to see if you can look at it from a different perspective. When you change the settings, you start to make trading more personal. When you make it more personal, it's better. It's as easy as that.

As you might have observed, it's almost impossible to see anything useful on that little picture. It's just a bunch of light-colored lines running up and down through the middle of the indicator window. Because these lines are overlapping, it looks like a heart monitor or an earthquake measuring device. It's hard to tell one line from the other.

But I felt like I had the essential elements I was looking for. I was happy with what I had, at least for starters. Remember, I didn't just want to see if a currency pair was overbought/oversold on the 1-minute chart. I wanted more: I wanted to know if it could go up so far, so fast, that it would end up being overbought/oversold on three time-frames simultaneously.

Stop and think about it for a moment: Doesn't it just seem more powerful, more exceptional, if a security goes to an extreme on three different time frames, rather than just one? It means that across the board, something has gone wacko. That's worth my attention. That's something I'd be interested in trading. So, while the overlapping lines gave me a headache, it was a good kind of headache — the kind you get when you're starting to think of something really cool and new.

It bears repeating: I don't want to look at the same shit that 99 out of 100 traders are looking at. You and I want to see something new and fresh and off the map. Most people would never think to consider a financial instrument oversold or overbought only if the condition existed on three time frames simultaneously. They don't think of this stuff, but it's not because they're dumb. I have never been the smartest trader in the room. I don't know any more than anyone else.

But it's true that if I create something different, I'm more likely to stick with it. If I use the Stochastic Oscillator off the shelf, with no unique twist, I'm not very likely to dedicate myself to its application. It's boring to do the same thing as everyone else (and, as we know, it's also financially dangerous). When we look at something from an innovative angle, it's special. It means something to me. I didn't invent the Stochastic, but I applied it differently. So what if you and I aren't rocket scientists? You can still dream big, and you can still do some impressive things. And it's simply easier to do great things when you're doing them on your own terms. That's why we became traders in the first place.

Think of people who have made a difference in the world. Think big. Steve Jobs. John Lennon and Paul McCartney. Jesus. The guy who invented hot dogs on a stick or two-ply toilet paper. These people took the tools at their disposal — stuff that pretty much anyone had access to — and did something special. And I'm sure it was easier to get up in the morning and do the hard work necessary to achieve greatness when they were working on something that hadn't been done before.

I humbly suggest that the Wallaby can do that for you. It's not the Holy Grail. It's not even the Righteous Grail, or the Reformed Grail — or even the I-Promise-To-Do-Better Grail. But it is different. I think you'll find that it's fun. And what we enjoy doing, we do better, because we're willing to do the work.

Rob, There's Still a Problem

Even though I'd spent the time to build the indicator, and I thought it looked pretty cool, there was a problem. We've already mentioned it: The problem was that the indicator, with all the crazy, jagged lines all over the place, was just too difficult to see clearly.

How I Solved the Problem I Just Mentioned

With the help of a friend, I decided to average out the Wallaby lines on the indicator, so that we could see what was going on with just one line. This one line would represent an average of the other three lines. It would represent the beans in our four-layer Mexican indicator dip. You know, beans provide the gas, and that's what our "average" line would do — it would provide the gas for the entire trading method.

Here's what the average line looks like:

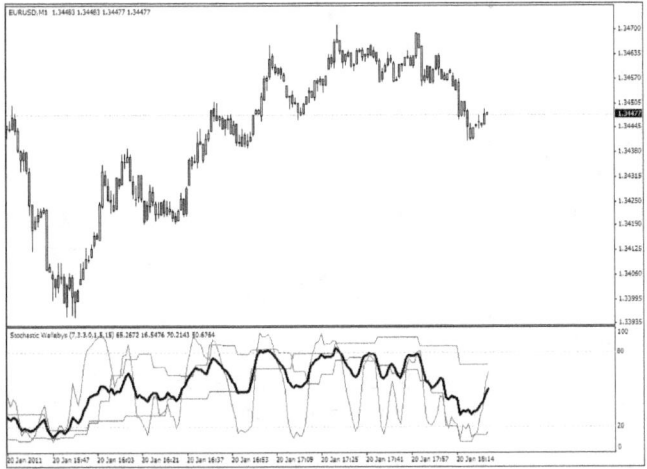

FIG. 1-7: The Wallaby, cleaned up.

Once this black line appeared on the chart, it all became simpler. In fact, once I had the average line up on the indicator, I didn't need the other lines at all. So I ditched them. I called that average line "the Wallaby line," and now, because it was easy to read and packed three time-frames' worth of information into one simple line, I was perfectly happy. And ready to go to work.

Want to see it?

FIG. 1-8: The Wallaby. It's the shiz-bombiest!

And now you know what the Wallaby is. And why I built it. And what it looks like. Now let's see what it can do.[4]

4. By the way, all the examples of the Wallaby on the charts in this book are taken from the latest iteration of the indicator, built by my friend Tega-San in Japan. You're seeing the Metatrader charts, which I use to plot the currencies and some futures contracts. And yes, the indicator is free, and you can get it on the Web site at: WallabyTrade.com.

*You can get the Wallaby indicator for a number of charting programs for free, by visiting **WallabyTrade.com**. But you don't even need the Wallaby indicator. If you can't get the indicator on your charts, just do the following: Add the regular Stochastic Oscillator set to 30, 10, 10; or the Relative Strength Index (RSI) set to 22, and you'll be on your way. Although these aren't perfect substitutions for the Wallaby indicator, they will do just fine. Really.*

2

Chapter Two

What can this Wallaby do?

Before I tell you what the Wallaby can do, I need to be totally up front about what it cannot do.

It cannot:

Turn back the clock so you can ask Katherine McDonald to the prom.

Speed up the timeline for The Rapture (Take me, Jesus!).

Make Geddy Lee not sound like a dying cow (sorry, Rush fans).

Here Are Some Things the Wallaby Can Do

You don't have to set up the Wallaby with the 1-minute, 5-minute and 15-minute charts. Let's run through the different settings you can use.

Type of Trading	Wallaby Settings	Timeframe Watch	Trade Length
Short-term	1, 5, 15	15	1 day
Medium-term	15, 60, 240	1530	3 days
Long-term	240, 1440, 10080	240	1 week

TABLE 2-1

Table 2.1 is meant to help you get started setting up your Wallaby. If you're interested in short-term trading, then I'd suggest setting the Wallaby indicator to show the 1-, 5- and 15-minute Stochastic Oscillators.

In Figure 2.1 I'll show you what my settings box looks like when I set up the Wallaby on my charts using the Metatrader charting platform — a free and easy-to-use program. Refer to Appendix One for more information about setting up your charts.[1]

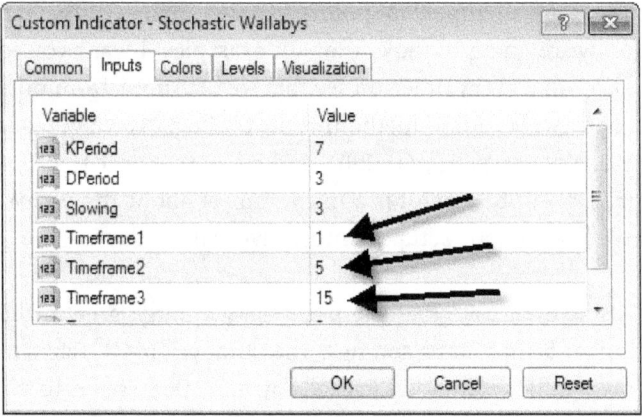

FIG. 2-1: Wallaby settings in Metatrader.

Now, assuming you've decided to do short-term trading and you've got your Wallaby set up with the right time frames, next you need to know which time-frame chart to watch for the trades. That's the next column. For example, if I've set myself up for short-term trading using the 1-minute, 5-minute, and 15-minute settings, then

---

1. The Wallaby indicator is available for free for a variety of charting platforms. See Appendix One for more information.

I keep either my 1- or 5-minute chart open and in front of me, in order to watch for and take the trade. The last column lets you know how long trades typically stay open. Incidentally, this is the average length of time between trade setups, as well.

These are all important points to remember, because later on we're going to look at lots of examples. I want you to know that every time you see that we're using a 15-minute chart, we're doing medium-term trading. We've got our Wallaby set to 15, 60, 240, and we can expect that our trades will be open for a maximum of about three days. We'll get a trade setup (at most) every three days.

Also, you'll note that the numbers get fairly large in the longer-term trading settings. The number "1440" refers to the number of minutes in each day, and 10080 refers to the number of minutes in each week. Simply put, I'm using minutes to display a full day or week.

3

Chapter Three

Bullish
Divergence

Divergence is easy. And it's powerful. I've been trading for 10 years, and it still exhilarates me. To start us off, I'll share a fun flip book-style drawing. In the upper-right corner of this book, on the next 100 pages, you'll see an expertly drawn little man. He looks like this:

Flip through the pages right now, paying attention to the animation. Super high-tech, right? I am probably the first author to embed video to a regular, old-school book. If you thought video on the World Wide Web was huge, wait until you see how this takes off! ... All right, maybe not.

As you flip through the pages, you'll see the little man tossing the ball up into the air. Something special happens when the ball rises to the top of the arc. Do you notice it?

I'm sure you did: Even though the ball has gone higher, its speed has decreased. It's moving higher but not as quickly. We'll call this phenomenon a "lack of momentum."

You know when the ball gets up there at the top — reaching its zenith — that it's going to fall. As it turns over (also what I call "rolling over"), it's going slower now. Gravity becomes more powerful than the force that propelled it upward. It has run out of gas. These are signs that the initial trajectory has encountered an obstacle (in this case, the laws of nature). If you've got a small animal or a rotten piece of fruit nearby, go ahead and throw it straight up into the air and try this out. Please also clean up after yourself.

If you are a betting man (or woman, of course), you'd bet that the rotten dead animal you launched into the air was going to drop when it reached the top of its arc. And without something to catch its fall, such as your hand, it would fall all the way to the Earth, just like the ball does in our little animation. You'd also wager that the speed with which the dead creature is going to fall increases as it drops. That's all easy to understand, because everyone has seen an object go up into the air and then fall back down to the ground ... especially any of you who have seen Alex Smith play quarterback for the San Francisco 49ers. That was a joke. Okay, no it wasn't.

In the trading world, the same thing happens. Financial instruments act just like the ball. Take, for instance, the EUR/USD currency pair. It's my favorite rotten animal. Here's a chart:

FIG. 3-1: An upward trend

Above we observe the EUR/USD moving higher and
higher, in what most people call a trend — higher highs,
higher lows — that kind of stuff. Remember, as they say,
the trend is your friend. Trade with the trend. Be the trend.
Blah Blah. You know the drill.

But if the EUR/USD is the ball (or rotten animal) from
our example, then it is prone to the same forces of nature
as any rising object. It will drop. Even a currency pair
suspended in outer space by the forces of the Federal
Reserve (Quantitative Easing) or a jobs report (such as
the infamous Non Farm Egg Roll Report) eventually
succumbs to what I affectionately call "Financial Gravity."[1]

The remaining question is: How, pray tell, will we know when EUR/USD reaches the critical point at which it begins to turn? Sure, we know that it must eventually relax, fall, retrace, correct and so forth. What kinds of tools stand ready to broadcast the news that this trend might end? I present to you, Dear Reader, a partial list:

Candle patterns (see my friend, Steve Nison, about that);

Bollinger Bands (see Kathy Lien's "Little Book of Currency Trading" for a great chapter on the bands);

Moving Average Convergence Divergence, the Momentum Indicator, the Commodity Channel Index;

"Flow analysis" (whatever the hell that is – follow @fxflow on Twitter for the Down Low on this business);

Straight-up economic analysis, such as reading annual reports, financial statements, and parsing government economic reports;

And, because I know some of you do this — there's the Psychic Friends Network (when all else fails, as they say, consult an astrologer).

Each one of the items listed above is a tool. Each is a common method. Thousands of traders use these (and other) tools to set up trades. For every one thing I've listed above, there exist 100 additional indicators or chart

---

1. If you have a currency pair that stays up for four hours or more, call a doctor immediately. This is a "Viagra Candle," and it's not to be toyed with (for more than four hours, anyway).

doohickeys that traders buy, rent or worship. Each tool is simply a lens through which to look at the markets. They are equally useful, or worthless, depending on who you are and what you want out of the market. Really. Endless debates rage on about The Best Technique. Meanwhile, the debators continue to lose money just as easily as before. My personal favorite contribution to this purposeless debate is the idea of having an actual monkey make stock picks and then compare it to a portfolio run by a professional. You can already guess who I think would do better.

Let's Get Back to the Ball/
Rotten Animal Flying in the Air

All right, then. How does the ball relate to the EUR/USD chart shown previously? How can we see that a security has reached a point where it slows its rate of change upward?

The Wallaby, of course. That's my preferred method, anyway, and I plan on convincing you in the next 150 pages that you should enslave yourself to it for eternity. Or at least start a church in its honor or something. The best thing about pledging your undying allegiance to the Wallaby is that it won't require you to build pyramids or mercilessly slaughter all the little Jedi knights in the temple.[2]

FIG. 3-2: OMG

The Wallaby will require you, of course, to learn how to identify bearish divergence. The best part: It's as simple as it is powerful, and over the next few pages, I'll show you how to do it in three easy steps. So let's get this show on the road.

How to Identify Bearish Divergence

This will be the easiest thing you ever did. Even easier, Men, than learning those teenage, nocturnal discoveries of self-gratification.[3]

---

2. Thank you, @huckspin from Twitter, for the Jedi Wallaby picture. For another "Star Wars" Wallaby, turn to page 121.6.

3. However, learning to identify bearish divergence will not cause blindness or damn you to hell. These are reasons you might consider trading divergence as an alternative.

In the next few paragraphs, combined with a few images, I will show you how to identify bearish divergence. I'm going to ask you to play along and even do the unthinkable act of drawing inside this book, which, when I was a kid, was grounds for a good spanking. But my babysitter was hot, so it was totally worth it. (I found myself ripping pages from books every time she came over. Not really.)

The first thing we'll do is show a EUR/USD chart again, this time adding just one more Stochastic Indicator. Then a few words to clarify what we're looking at. I promised you three steps, but we've got to see this damn chart first. And then I promise we'll proceed with the steps.

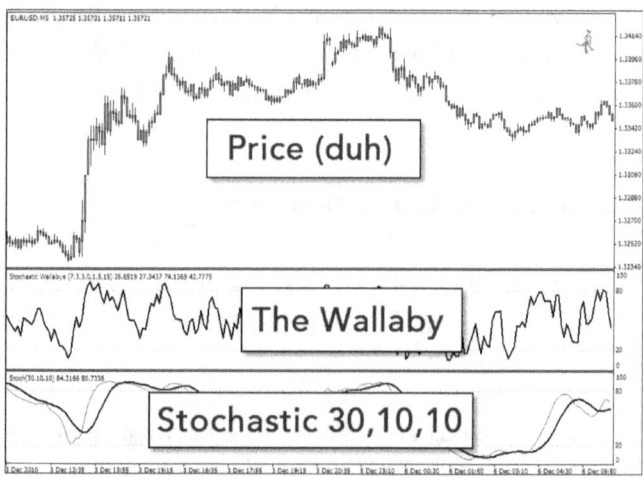

FIG. 3-3: Chart elements

If you have any questions about what you see on the above chart, then just flip to the back of this book to the Appendix One, entitled "Setting Up Your Charts," and you'll get the whole story. Reading the entire section requires just five short minutes of your time. It's worth ten minutes if you're confused in any way about what you see. Or if you want to know how to obtain the Wallaby indicator for your charts.

In Figure 3-3 we see price (the candles – which I use instead of bar or line charts), the Wallaby Indicator and the regular-flavor Stochastic Oscillator set to 30, 10, 10. Time for the three steps.

Step One

Find two high points on the chart. I don't care where you look first. Really. Start from the left or the right. I just want you to identify any points that you could call "highest" on the chart. Then circle these points with a pencil. Go ahead right now and do the circling on the EUR/USD chart above. If you don't have a pencil, you are welcome to just circle the area on the chart with your finger. When you're finished, it probably ought to look something like this:

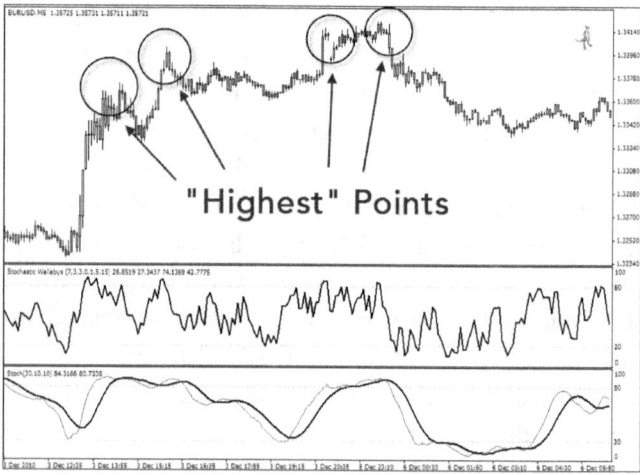

FIG. 3-4: These points are high

It will not help you draw better circles on the high points if you're stoned or inebriated. Actually, if you've been smoking dope while reading this book, this is what your chart probably looks like now:

So please put down the doobie and get back to work.
You're actually almost finished with Step One, but there's
one more thing we need to do ... we need to:

DRAW A VERTICAL LINE FROM THE HIGH PEAKS
DOWN TO THE REGULAR STOCHASTIC LINES.

I wrote that in capital letters to make sure you understand
what I'm asking you to do. Please take a moment and
use your pencil, and do it right now. Draw a straight line
down from each peak, connecting that line to the regular
Stochastic Oscillator lines below. Here's what it will look
like:

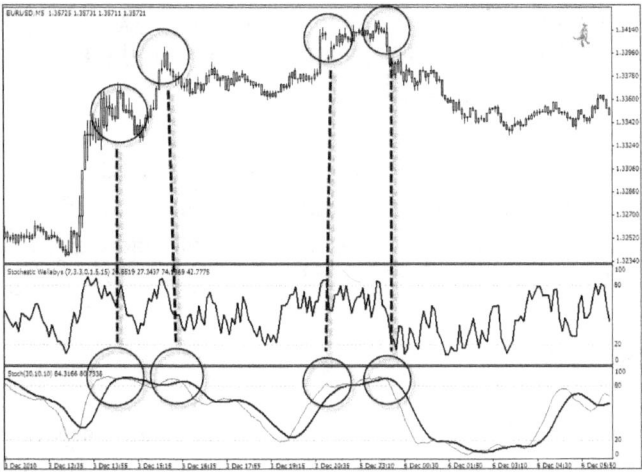

FIG. 3-5: Connecting the peaks

We just did this so we can find out if each peak was overbought on the Stochastic Oscillator. In this example above, the answer is yes, they're all overbought. How do we know that? Because the Stochastic Line is above the top line — the 80 line — on the indicator. That's overbought. And as you'll remember, that means that price has become overextended to the upside and could be ready for a substantial drop. Perhaps, as we've said, the ball is ready to fall.

Let's lay out Step One in a single sentence. Here goes:

Wallaby Bearish Divergence Step One:

Going from left to right, find at least two separate peaks in price which are also each overbought on the Regular Stochastic Oscillator, set to 30, 10, 10.

You've just completed Step One. If you've read this far, then there's no turning back. You simply have to read Step Two, because this is where things get wild and crazy. It's arts and crafts time!

Step Two

All right, I lied. It's not going to get wild and crazy, but you're more than one-third of the way through the steps, so keep going!

The next step is as simple. Take your special Wallaby Brand Hi-Tec Writing Device® and your Wallaby Brand Measuring Stick Thingy® and place the Measuring Stick (commonly known as a "ruler," but I hate Rulers, and I hate Royalty of any kind, so I'm not using that word) and draw a line over the tops of the candles moving upward on the EUR/USD chart. Please do it on the chart above, and please do it right now.[4]

When you're done, it should look like this:

FIG. 3-6: Trendline across the high points.

4. If you didn't get a Wallaby Brand Hi-Tec Writing Device® or a Wallaby Brand Measuring Stick Thingy® with your book — which are available as part of the Wallaby Box Set of Books® — then you can just prick your finger with a needle and use your blood as a pen, and cut out your tibia bone and use that as a ruler. Seems completely reasonable.

Hey! You're a genius. I'm going to call your mom and tell her how well you've done. In fact, you just completed Step Two!

But in order to ensure that I've taken something simple and turned into a complicated nightmare that's impossible to remember, I've written out a longish description of this Second, Very Important Step, and here it is:

Wallaby Bearish Divergence Step Two:

Draw a trendline above the candles, from left to right, connecting the two peaks from Step One, using the highest candle wicks as starting and ending points.

That's Step Two, and we're almost finished.

Just so you know, at the end of the chapter, I'll re-write all three rules in one place. Also, if you bought the box set of books (from my Web site), you've got a Wallaby Divergence Special Notecard Cheat Sheet® with all the rules, and you've probably already posted that next to your computer.

Step Three

Next we need to draw a trendline on the Wallaby Indicator — and we're going to do it in such a way so that we can compare the line we drew on price with the line we've drawn on the Wallaby. As you can imagine, we're going to compare the slopes of the two lines.

To do this, please go back to the previous chart for the EUR/USD, Figure 3.6, and draw a vertical line down, starting at the exact beginning point of the trendline you drew on the candles, and ending at the red Wallaby Indicator line. Call this point "1." Why are we doing this? To set up the precise position where we'll start our trendline on the Wallaby. We want it to begin directly below the starting point of the trendline on the price.

Next draw another vertical line downward, starting at the exact ending point of the trendline you drew on the candles, and terminate your new vertical line at the red Wallaby line. We'll call this point "2." When you've completed your masterpiece of vertical lines, the chart should look something like this:

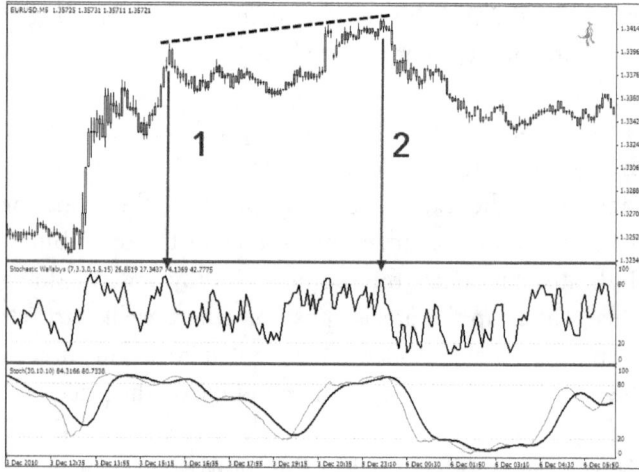

FIG. 3-7: Nice vertical lines!

You're doing great. This isn't difficult at all, is it? Some of you are just flying through this section (you know, the A and B students from high school geometry: What is the circumference of the square root of the quadratic diameter of a hexagonal arthropod? Why, it's orange, of course!).

As noted a moment ago, these vertical lines can presently serve as our starting and ending points for a trendline on the Wallaby Indicator. Your starting point is the vertical line on the left, or point "1." Your ending point is the vertical line on the right — point "2." Please take a moment now, and with your own blood, draw a line across the top of the red Wallaby Indicator, from left to right. When you're finished, it should look like this:

FIG. 3-8: Nice blood stains!

On second thought, let's not draw the trendline with your blood; instead, let's just use a regular pen like normal people. Here's what it should look like:

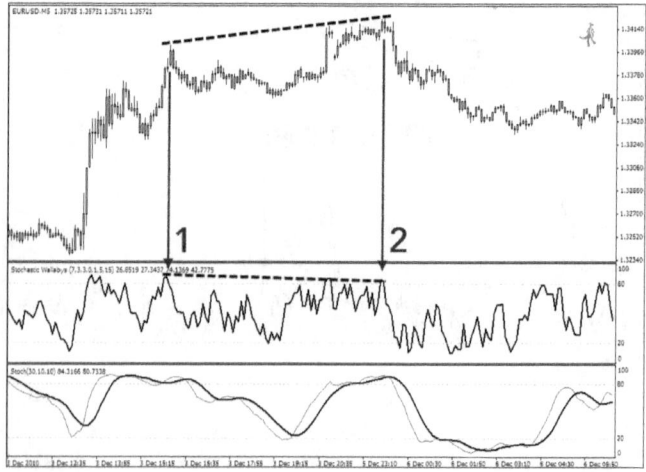

FIG. 3-9: Well done!

You've now got a trendline on the Wallaby Indicator. Let's summarize Step Three and then you can tie up a tourniquet and stop the flow of blood from your wounds created by Figure 3-8.

Wallaby Bearish Divergence Step Three:

Draw a trendline on the Wallaby Indicator using the trendline on the price (candles/bars) for starting and ending reference points.

My favorite part is next: We're now ready to bring this all together. I'll summarize the three steps for us, and then give Regular Wallaby Bearish Divergence a definition.

Wallaby Bearish Divergence Step One:

Going from left to right, find two separate peaks in price which are also each overbought on the Regular Stochastic Oscillator, set to 30, 10, 10.

Wallaby Bearish Divergence Step Two:

Draw a trendline above the candles, from left to right, connecting the two peaks from Step One, using the highest candle wicks as starting and ending points.

Wallaby Bearish Divergence Step Three:

Draw a trendline on the Wallaby Indicator using the trendline on the price (candles/bars) for starting and ending reference points.

And once we finish these three steps, identifying Regular Wallaby Bearish Divergence is easy.

REGULAR BEARISH WALLABY DIVERGENCE:

Regular bearish divergence exists when:

a) A security produces higher highs in price.

b) These highs are also simultaneously overbought on the regular Stochastic Oscillator set to 30, 10, 10.

c) And the Wallaby Indicator, over the exact same period of time, produces lower highs.

That's it. Using this as a definition, do we see bearish divergence on the EUR/USD in the charts from this chapter? Well, for starters, it would have been a massive waste of your time to do all this work and then answer the question with a "no." So you can probably already guess that the answer is yes. But can you see why the answer is yes? Let me show you one more chart and explain visually why the answer is yes:

FIG. 3-10: Points 1 and 2 show bearish divergence.

It's clear from Figure 3-10 that we have regular bearish divergence. We call it "regular" because there are other kinds of divergence (which we'll cover later). We call it "bearish" because the occurrence of this phenomenon means that price is probably soon heading lower (that's bearish). We call it "divergence" because what price is doing is different (divergent) from what the indicator is doing.

To summarize this again, to make sure that it's totally and completely clear — we have just compared what price is doing (going higher) with what the Stochastic Oscillator on three different time-frame charts is doing (going lower). The fact that price is able to jump a bit higher, but the indicator can't keep up — that fact just by itself is a sign that something has gone wrong. The fact that the Stochastic Oscillator across three time-frame charts failed to confirm the new highs is important. It's more powerful than if we simply showed one oscillator by itself and made the comparison.

Why is this happening to the EUR/USD at this exact point in time? Maybe people are less excited about buying the pair because a major economic announcement is due for release. Maybe there is still buying going on, but it's going on at a slower rate before the start of a holiday weekend. Maybe there are fewer people out there willing to send the EUR/USD higher because the data coming out of Europe is now only perceived to be slightly better than the economic numbers coming out of the United States. Maybe some trend-traders are starting to take their profits. Whatever the underlying cause, it's there, right in front of us. And it means something. It means that we're interested in finding a way to sell this currency pair.

We're even more interested in selling the currency pair because these peaks on price aren't just progressively higher, but they're also overbought on the regular, old Stochastic Oscillator. Did you forget that we originally took notice of the overbought status of the Stochastic in the lower panel of the chart? Go back to Step One and Figure 3-5 if you need a reminder (don't worry, we won't continue without you).

Of all the traders who look at divergence, 99% do not incorporate this overbought requirement into the analysis. Over time you'll find that it can make a substantial difference and filters out some of the trades you really don't want to take.

Next, we're going to take a look at what our Wallaby superhero is up to.

By now some of you have wondered if there are possibly some different places to draw your trendlines on the candles and the Wallaby Indicator. The answer is yes. In these charts, you actually could have drawn the trendlines starting a little bit earlier and ending a little bit earlier — and I want you to know that it would have been perfectly fine to do so. We're not talking about an exact science here, and there's plenty of wiggle room. Later on we'll look at lots more examples that will show you how flexible we can be with drawing these lines.

4

Chapter Four

Bearish
Divergence

Because you're now an expert in bearish divergence, we can do something interesting in this chapter (instead of taking you through a long and boring history of how King James commissioned 75 monks to starve themselves while transcribing the ancient Wallaby scrolls onto parchment, using only Koala blood as ink and their untrimmed fingernails as pens).

And so you ask, what is that very interesting thing that we're going to do instead of the long and boring crap?

I'm going to show you a Wallaby trade, start to finish, to sort of whet your appetite for more. Yeah, you heard me. Here's why I want to show you one complete trade, right now: I want you to finish this book in one sitting. I want you to keep moving forward. And by showing you the good stuff — an entire trade — I think you'll be motivated to discover the other really good stuff that's coming later in the book. Also, if your eyeballs finish reading the book soon, you're more likely to do something with the information you've learned. If you use the information, you're more likely to learn it better. The better you learn it, the better you'll be at trading it. And trading it is, well, the most fun I've ever had on the short-term charts. And helping you to trade more profitably is the entire point of this book.

I'll shut up now, and we're going to launch up to the next level. Here's a chart of a bullish divergence Wallaby setup, from start to finish.

FIG. 4-1: A Wallaby buy trade from start to finish.

What's happening in Figure 4-1? First, the EUR/USD made lower lows on price — you can see that along the trendline I drew beneath the candles. Across that same period of time, the currency pair was oversold on the regular Stochastic Oscillator set to 30,10,10. (I've pointed this out by enclosing these areas in boxes at the bottom of the chart.) Last of all, the Wallaby Stochastic, over this same period of time, was making higher lows. To sum it up: The currency pair was stretching lower on price, but the Wallaby Indicator just couldn't agree to follow. It wanted to go up.

That's bullish divergence, Friends, and it was an early warning sign that the EUR/USD could be headed upward next. And that's what it did — 50 points worth of movement within the next couple of hours. As indicated by the arrows, we bought near the very bottom and then we sold when the currency pair had risen by about 50 pips. I'll describe the method for entering and exiting the trades in later chapters. But this is what a trade looks like from start to finish. It's a standard Wallaby trade when things go well.

Some of you have already seen everything you need to see about bullish divergence for now. If you feel completely comfortable with the concept, feel free to skip ahead to the next chapter. However, I'd recommend that you stick around. It's only a few pages, and I promise it will be worth your time, as well as entertaining.

For the rest of the examples in this chapter, I'm going to use the S&P 500 index (cash) for charting examples. But don't forget, everything we're talking about here is as applicable to stocks, currencies, futures, precious metals, bonds and anything else you can trade.[1]

Identifying Regular Bullish Divergence

Three steps is all it takes. With the foundation you already have from the previous chart, we can breeze through each one of them.

---

1. For more information on which financial instruments have traditionally worked well with the Wallaby Indicator, see Appendix Six in the back of the book.

Wallaby Bullish Divergence Step One:

Going from left to right, find two separate valleys in price that are also each oversold on the Regular Stochastic Oscillator, set to 30,10,10.

You're clearly aware that all we've done is reversed the first step from the previous chapter. We want to see that price has been able to make new lows. We also want to know that those lows are oversold, thus indicating that the pair is flying out of control in a downward move. I've gone ahead and prepared a chart for us:

FIG. 4-2: S&P 500 makes lower lows that are oversold.

I've drawn arrows on the chart in Figure 4-2 so you can see that low points #1 and #2 are each oversold on the regular Stochastic Oscillator. Do you notice that these two valleys of oversold candles are separate and distinct? By that, I mean that at point #1, the index went oversold and then jumped up out of oversold, and then in point #2 dipped back down into oversold territory? That's important to me. For a standard Wallaby trade, I want to see two distinct points that are each oversold before I'm ready to set up a divergence trade (and that goes for both bullish and bearish divergence). [FOOTNOTE: For those of you who are wondering, there are in fact non-standard Wallaby trades, and in these cases we don't require two separate overbought or oversold sets of candles. We'll talk about these trades in a later chapter. ENDFOOTNOTE]

And onward to Step Two:

Wallaby Bullish Divergence Step Two:

Draw a trendline above the candles, from left to right, connecting the two peaks from Step One using the highest candle wicks as a starting and ending point.

That's easy enough, right? I've got the chart ready, and here it is:

FIG. 4-3: Trendline in place!

Simple, right? You're just zooming through these rules. No reason we can't just fly into the next one.

Wallaby Bullish Divergence Step Three:

Draw a trendline on the Wallaby Indicator using the trendline on the candles above for starting and ending reference points.

I've got this chart ready, too. Before I show it to you, I want to prepare you for something: There are lots of different ways to draw trendlines on these charts and what you would draw may look different from what I draw. Most of the time, my charts and your charts are going to look very similar. But there are times when they don't. That's okay. The differences are usually very minimal. Also, please keep in mind that while I've included as many charts as possible in the book, I've posted hundreds more charts online so you can see the various ways it's possible to set up the trades.

Here's the chart:

FIG. 4-4: Trendline on the Wallaby.

Can you see that while the S&P 500 is falling from point #1 to point #2, the Wallaby is rising? That's what we like to see.

Next take a closer look at area #2. Just within that small zone, the price makes two rapid new lows in succession. Each time it falls in area #2, it gets just a bit lower. But the Wallaby in that same period of time rises — even across a small number of candles. I'm going to pause and actually point this out on a chart.

FIG. 4-4: A closer look at area #2

So, is the S&P 500 index bullish divergent in Figure 4-4? You bet it is! It's not only bullish divergent across points

#1 and #2, but it's also bullish divergent across a smaller number of candles in area #2.[2]

Let's do a quick review.

REGULAR BULLISH WALLABY DIVERGENCE:

Regular bullish divergence exists when:

a) A security produces lower lows in price.
b) These lows are also simultaneously oversold on the regular Stochastic Oscillator, set to 30,10,10.
The Wallaby Indicator, over the exact same period of time, produces higher lows.

Figure 4-4 clearly shows this phenomenon across points #1 and #2. The index went lower on price but failed to do the same on the Wallaby Indicator. We love that! It shows reduced enthusiasm for selling the pair. And that's natural, right? I mean, at some point the buyers dry up and people start to think, "Holy crap! The S&P has fallen a lot today. I'm going to start taking profits." At the same time these traders are exiting profitable shorts (by purchasing the index), other traders start to notice that they'd like to buy the S&P because it's "on sale." As they buy it, the short-sellers who didn't already get out begin to have their stops

---

1. The only reason I brought this up is because I knew some of you were going to ask, and then start to wonder.

triggered. That brings the index up a bit higher as well. Of course, this is all a generalization of the story behind the trade, but you get the idea. Shorts are getting squeezed out, buyers are coming into the market and the index starts to rise.

This type of trade setup can often occur later in the trading sessions (or even in after-hours trading on the futures market), when all the craziness has subsided and binge sellers have passed out on the street, drunken with the sweet, intoxicating aroma of a stock index marinated in the blood of a thousand short-sellers. You, however, may have stayed on the sidelines for the entire trading session, just watching this downward move play out, wondering if you'll get the chance to trade a divergence setup. And you do. Patience pays off. Staying out of the market and waiting for a setup is one of the most enjoyable things a Wallaby trader does.

Often smart traders will ask me if there is a way to capture that entire move downward and trade with that short-term daily trend — and then jump in and go the other way when the Wallaby trade sets up. The answer is yes, of course; there was most likely a bearish Wallaby trade previously that led to all this wild selling. So there's no reason why you wouldn't have been able to (occasionally) ride the move down and then get yourself geared up to go the other way. Some traders are better at doing that than others. It requires a lot of screen time.

Here is a summary of the rules, all in one place for you:

Wallaby Bullish Divergence Step One:

Going from left to right, find two separate valleys in price that are also each oversold on the Regular Stochastic Oscillator, set to 30,10,10.

Wallaby Bullish Divergence Step Two:

Draw a trendline above the candles, from left to right, connecting the two peaks from Step One using the highest candle wicks as a starting and ending point.

Wallaby Bullish Divergence Step Three:

Draw a trendline on the Wallaby Indicator using the trendline on the candles above for starting and ending reference points.

And, to review:

REGULAR BULLISH WALLABY DIVERGENCE:

Regular bullish divergence exists when:

a) A security produces lower lows in price.
b) These lows are also simultaneously oversold on the regular Stochastic Oscillator, set to 30,10,10.

And the Wallaby Indicator, over the exact same period of time, produces higher lows.

When this happens, we're going to think about setting up a buy trade.

In the next chapter, I'm going to show you why women are better traders than men ... at least, if I've got enough time to talk about that, during the course of a discussion about bending the Wallaby rules. Right now, you've got the basics. You can identify regular bearish and regular bullish Wallaby divergence. You're on the road to taking some really good trades, but that's not everything. You haven't learned how to bend the rules yet. And once you learn how to bend the rules, you open an entire new level of Wallaby trading, with twice the opportunities for trading, and some of the very best, most profitable, most exciting Wallaby trades.

5

Chapter Five

Bending the Divergence Rules

I once lost a job because I didn't realize we were supposed to come to work every day. One Tuesday I walked in around 10:31 in the morning, bagel and newspaper in hand, wiping the tired, crusty sand out of my bloodshot eyes, walking past the cubes of death, and someone said, "Hey, Booker, where were you yesterday?" The rest of the exchange went something like this:

ME: I didn't come in yesterday because I needed a day to think.

INCREDULOUS LEMMING: Well, um, that's kind of odd.

ME: What's odd?

I.L.: Taking a day off work just to think.

ME: Well, like, what would you advise me to do when I need a day to think deeply about some things? This place stifles every last molecule of creativity in humans. The florescent lights, the reality that we're all boxed into a small workspace, the lack of any music or background noise. Have you ever noticed that you never hear laughing out loud in the office? And why is everything here light brown?

I.L.: Um, I don't know how to respond to that. Sure, all those things are true about the office, but what am I going to do about it? Why not just wait for the weekend for some of that downtime? Or lunch?

ME: It's easier for me to think in Las Vegas.

I.L.: Wait a minute — you went to Las Vegas?

ME: Yeah. You should have come. It was a riot.

I.L.: I couldn't do that! I have to work!

ME: Wait. Are you telling me that everyone here comes in every day?

It still shocks me that employers expect you to come to work every weekday, even if you know you're going to be unproductive and have better things to do. A day off now and then to recharge, watch some Netflix, give yourself an extra day in the same underwear — you can call it a day off, but I'd rather call it a "day on." If you say that not coming to work is a day off, what you're really saying is that you're only really "on" while you're at work. That's insane and you know it.

At that same job, which lasted for a few months, I also wore jeans to work every day, except Friday, just to be a jackass about the dress code. On Fridays I'd wear a full suit or a blue chiffon tuxedo.[1] I also refused to wear underwear.[2]

---

1. Not actually true.
2. Actually true.

And once I completely covered a woman's cubicle in photos of Mario Lopez printed off from the giant printer (what else would that thing be used for?).

For these innocent violations of Regular Employee Policy Bible Code, I got my desk moved to the area right outside of Human Resources, where they could keep an eye on me. Fortunately, this desk was also in the main traffic line where people traveled in order to get to the bathroom and the break room. Needless to say, within a couple of days, I had an extra-comfortable chair, a television and a steady stream of guests over in my area all day long. Work wasn't so bad after all.[3]

I just told you that story to introduce the concept of bending the rules.

Bending the rules can be fun, and when we're talking about the Wallaby trade, it can also be profitable. In the next few chart examples, I want to show you some ways in which Wallaby divergence doesn't set up exactly right, but it's still worth calling divergence for the purpose of getting a trade.

---

3. Also, for the record, I stayed up late and worked at night when everyone was gone. I put in more than 10 hours a day, easily, and I worked every single weekend. I missed my high school and law school reunions for work-related trips. And, last of all, I loved those people. I still miss you all every day. Hi, Carrie, Mark, Will, Heidi, Andrew, Todd, Jon, Chris, Matt, Amanda, Lonnie, Genny, Chaz, Ryan and Ken!

Just so you know ahead of time, whenever we see a problematic Wallaby trade — something that bends or breaks the rules — we're going to call it Wallaby "Pervergence." That's because for some reason, the Wallaby setup has been perverted. Something is wrong with it, in other words. But we're still going to take it. One by one, let's consider the different types of problems you'll see with Wallaby setups.[4]

Divergence Problem #1: Not Oversold or Overbought

Sometimes the regular Stochastic Oscillator just doesn't go oversold or overbought all the way. And everything else about the divergence setup looks perfect. In a situation like this, we're going to bend the rules and give our stamp of approval to the setup.

In this first chart, the S&P doesn't quite get overbought on the right side of the setup:

---

4. Thanks, Max. You invented the term "Pervergence," and I've always been grateful for your creativity and humor. Gluten Morgen! (That means "have a pastry for breakfast" in German.)

FIG. 5-1: Not overbought at position #2. That's okay!

I've drawn a box over the area in question, so you can see that neither of the Stochastic lines goes above 80 at position #2. But look at what else we have going for the setup: The index is clearly making higher highs on price from point #1 to point #2, and it's making lower highs on the Wallaby Indicator across the same two points in time. Is it bending the rules to say this is Wallaby divergence? Yes! We're in clear violation of Rule One — which states:

Wallaby Bearish Divergence Step One:

Going from left to right, find two separate peaks in price that are also each overbought on the regular Stochastic

Oscillator, set to 30,10,10.

We don't have two separate overbought peaks, and so we're breaking this rule. Or we're bending it. And I'm here to tell you that no matter what else I said previously in this book, I'm going to accept this setup as a bent-rules divergence trade. That's good enough.

Let's look at an example of this rule-bending on a bullish divergence chart:

FIG. 5-2: Not oversold at position #2. That's okay!

In Figure 5-2, the regular Stochastic doesn't go below 20 at position #2. It gets really close to reaching the 20 line but doesn't do it. Well, we're going to bend the rules. The Wallaby judges have decided that it's good enough.

Here's the principle you can follow when considering whether to accept a divergence setup when point #2 isn't quite overbought or oversold all the way:

Pervergence, Principle #1

If the regular Stochastic Oscillator is not oversold or overbought for point #2, does it at least get close? How extreme is the difference between the angle of the trendline on price versus the angle of the trendline on the Wallaby Indicator?

Divergence Problem #2: One Single Area of OB/OS

Sometimes a setup shows you that a financial instrument was able to go overbought or oversold — but it's not oversold or overbought across two points in time on the regular Stochastic. Here is what that looks like:

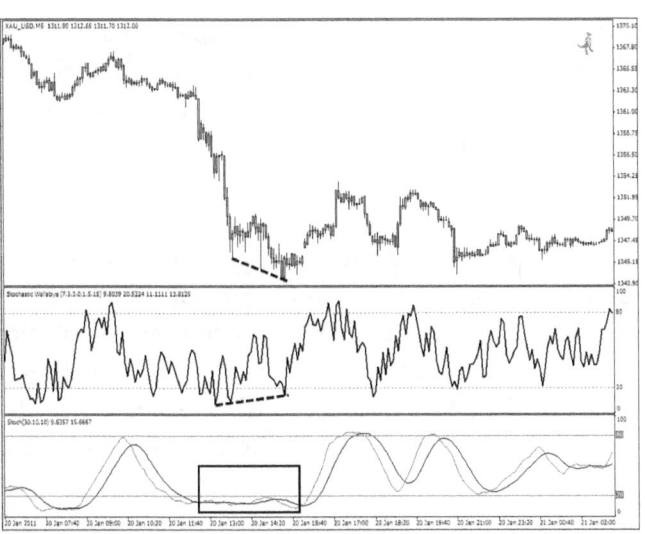

FIG. 5-3: One longish area of "oversold-ness."

The divergence is obvious — price is going lower, and at the same time, the Wallaby is going higher, and it's so clear that it's hard to resist getting involved. The Wallaby has two separate valleys (and in fact, it's got three). At the same time, the regular Stochastic is just in the depths of hell. One solid line just scraping along the bottom. You know from the rules in Chapter 4 that we'd like to see two separate and oversold valleys on the regular Stochastic. This chart doesn't have what the rules seem to require.

But is it justifiable? Can we call it Perverted Divergence and take a trade? To me there's one simple way to properly bend the rules in this case, and it means we need to drop down to a lower time-frame chart. Think about it: Over this same stretch of time on the 5-minute chart, there will be more candles on the 1-minute chart, and across this greater number of candles, maybe we'll see two separate oversold areas.

It bears repeating here: I want two separate overbought or oversold areas, or at least two separate valleys or peaks on the regular Stochastic. I'd prefer not to take a divergence trade without this condition being met. In order to meet this condition, then, we might need to switch to a shorter time-frame chart so we can see more candles. Here's the 1-minute chart:

FIG. 5-4: Presto! Two areas!

You can see in Figure 5-4 that our plan worked. Both points #1 and #2 are oversold on the regular Stochastic. From this point on, we can enter the trade and watch the lower time frame 1-minute chart. We've switched the time frame that we're going to look at. For me, this isn't half bad. We now get an earlier entry on the trade, which you'll learn later is very important to me.

For these reasons, I'd go ahead and say the divergence setup is valid on the 1-minute chart. The only way we were able to consider this trade is because we moved to a lower time-frame chart. You could do this for any time-frame chart, of course — you could have seen a "single area" problem setup on the 1-hour chart, and then moved down to the 15-minute chart to see if it looked any better. For now, let's just summarize the principle:

Pervergence, Principle #2

If all the elements of divergence appear, but across only one continuous area of overbought/oversold candles, it's appropriate to move to a lower time-frame chart (any lower time-frame chart) to see if the divergence appears across two separate overbought/oversold areas. Keep in mind that Pervergence Principle #2 can be used on this lower time-frame chart to "justify" the divergence.

Our final Pervergence Principle should cause the most controversy (like wearing jeans to work on a non-casual

Monday). Before you read this section, I'm already going to tell you that there will be people out there who say that this next section shows that we can break every rule we have previously discussed. And if we can break every rule we previously discussed, why do we have rules at all? Why do we have a Wallaby Indicator at all? If you're ready for a great example of Pervergence and my answer to the above questions, then you're ready for the next section.

Divergence Problem # 3: "Pervergence"

What if price and the Wallaby aren't really divergent? What if price is flat? What if the Wallaby is flat? It can happen. If price is flat but the Wallaby Stochastic clearly shows divergence, it's all right. But what if that is combined with all sorts of other Pervergent features? What then? We have Massive Pervergence, which frankly, just sounds gross. Let's take a look.

FIG. 5-5: Can you see all the problems on this chart?

Figure 5-5 has more problems than a jar of New York salsa in a Texas saloon.

One by one, let's discuss the four major problems on this chart.

Problem A: The price is actually flat across the candles that we're considering. You might recognize this as a "Double Bottom" formation. When we go looking for divergence, we want to see price rising or falling over time. How can we find divergence if price is moving flatly? I admit, it's hard to stomach. But stay with me, and think about this: Over the same stretch of time, at least the Wallaby Indicator is rising sharply. That's got to count for something. Believe me, you're going to find examples of this on the charts, and you're going to be tempted to justify a divergence setup. We might as well cover it, so if you do justify it, you at least know how to trade it.

Problem B: I've drawn a trendline straight through the Wallaby Indicator. I cut right through it, as if it doesn't matter at all. Why would I do such a thing? Well, I'm doing it to better highlight the fact that over this stretch of candles, the Wallaby is making higher lows, and it's very clear. I just have to draw on top of a line in order to do it. Just so you know — it's perfectly acceptable to draw your trendlines and cut through indicators or even candles. As long as you find divergence across price versus the Wallaby, it's okay that your trendline passes through some candles or some Wallaby lines. You'll see more examples of this later on.

Problem C: The regular Stochastic isn't really oversold on the exact, perfect spots. If you look closely, it's easy to see that Oil was oversold a few candles before the end of the trendline that we've drawn on the candles themselves. Remember, we'd like to line up the oversold points at exactly the same starting and ending points as the trendline on the price. But we didn't do that here. Is that acceptable? Why the hell not? We're breaking every other rule, and we're not even done!

Problem D: Our trendline on the Wallaby doesn't match with the trendline on price! We started drawing our trendline on the Wallaby Indicator earlier than where we started drawing it on the candles. Is this okay? Yeah, it's fine. What we're showing is still the same thing: Price is flat while the Wallaby is rising. We're bending the rules here, and we've done a ton of bending in a very short period of time, in just one chart.

And that's why we call this last example "Pervergence." It's perverted divergence — almost completely wacko to the point that most people would overlook it. But it turns out that this setup, although clearly deficient in some areas, produced an early warning sign that price was going to rise. And that's why we're here in the first place. It's just like work: They pay you to get stuff done, and they shouldn't be so ridiculous about the workplace rules. Sometimes the crazy people (and crazy setups) are just as good — or better — than the plain vanilla ones.

Here's a summary of the final principle:

Pervergence, Principle #3

"Pervergence" is perverted divergence. It's when there are multiple weak points in the divergence setup all at the same time, centering on or stemming from the fact that price is flat (or worse, going in the wrong direction) over the set of candles you're considering. Consider these trades as a whole — and pay special attention to the slope of the Wallaby trendline and the depth of the overbought/oversold condition on the chart.

Fair enough. Sometimes the setup looks crappy. Would anyone take the pervergence trade in Figure 5-5? Would this be acceptable at all? The answer is yes. You'll find that some of the bent-rules Wallaby divergence setups have multiple weak points all at the same time, and they're still worth trading. What makes it justifiable? How can we say that Figure 5-5 is a valid trade setup and not destroy everything we've worked so hard for so far in the book? The answer is simple: These Pervergence setups are not for everyone. You do not have to take them. They look crappy, and they have all sorts of deficiencies. They look like divergence, even though they don't comply with some of the divergence guidelines. Looking like divergence, as it turns out, can be good enough. But maybe it's not good enough for you.

Principle #3 above states that we consider the trade as a whole. We consider all the factors and then we step back, and we think in probabilistic terms. Is this something we've seen before in our testing? Are price and the Wallaby doing something different across one stretch of time? Many traders are uncomfortable with the thought of bending the rules, because once they bend some of the rules, they're afraid they're going to bend all the rules. Or they're afraid that once some rules have been bent, none of the rules apply in the first place. And this is all crap. No trading system is perfect, and every trading system has setups that exist on the edges of the rules. These are the trades that no one wants to talk about. Are they valid trades or not? What do they look like, and how do we handle them? That's what I am here to do: explain what happens on the edges of the rules and tell you what to do when something doesn't look quite right — but it doesn't look so terrible that you're going to walk away from the trade.

I find that these bent-rules setups — especially Pervergence — appear after economic news is released. That's when traders go berserk and start vomiting all over their keyboards. Wall Street and retail traders alike consume so much Tums/Valium/Viagra during the 15-minutes before and after the Non Farm Payroll report that they could open their own pharmacies. When things get a bit wild, a financial instrument might not make a new high or low. Right up until the moment the report is released, a divergence trade might be forming. And then BAM! The report is released, and there isn't any more time for the divergence trade to set up. We get what we get, and the market goes racing off into the distance. I want you to start seeing the early signs of divergence so that before these economic reports are released, you can see pieces of the puzzle fitting together. Even if you choose not to trade during the fury and madness of a Non Farm Payroll report, you at least can see the bigger picture. As my friend, Dirk du Toit, once told me, perspective is everything. Seeing the big picture, being able to stand back and get a view of things and sort them out — that's gold. That's where profitable traders are made.

You might consider reducing your trade size on a bent-rules trade by half, and then you won't be risking as much on a trade that didn't meet all the conditions for Wallaby divergence. You might consider passing on the first few bent-rules trades you see and just paper-trading these setups. That way you can get a feel for what they look like, how they act differently and how you can best take advantage of them. You might consider, on the other hand, only taking bent-rules trades. You might find that you become better at trading them than even the normal, "perfect-looking" setups.

But what does it even mean to "take" a Wallaby trade? Turn the page and find out.

6

Entering a Wallaby Trade

When I go to trading conferences, I hear people arguing all the time about whether the entry or exit for a trade is more important. I've engaged in such debate as well. This is like arguing about the name of God, or about whether or not a peanut butter and jelly sandwich would wear a one- or two-piece bathing suit. Sheezy-Weezy, people! Some pretty heated confrontations erupt when you get people on this subject, and at the end of the day, the truth is that they both matter. If you're a jackass about this topic, and you feel like arguing with me right now, just put this book down for a few minutes and collect yourself. We're not going to engage in any useless debates inside the pages of my book.

Now that we're on the same page, let's cover some important ground, starting with the basis for the entry of a Wallaby trade.

The Crossover Is the Entry

Take a look at this screen-shot of the regular Stochastic Oscillator. The arrow in the image points to the fast line on the oscillator as it crosses above the slower line:

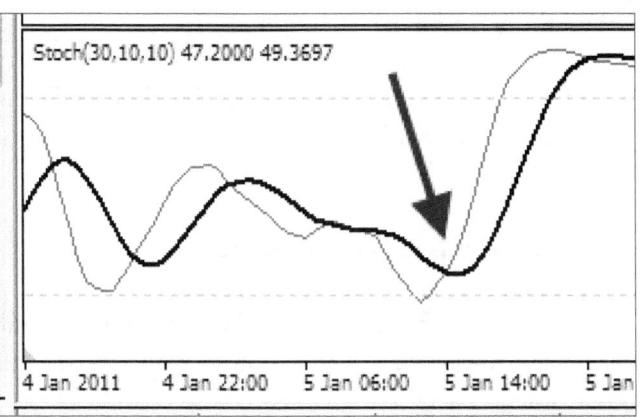

FIG. 6-1: Crossover, close up.

That's all you need to know about entering a Wallaby trade. Here are the rules:

Trade Entry for Bullish Divergence

ṡumoopṡeṡüt tüꞔccaꞔðelappropiꞔqüüṡ
 coꞔgrüo per a pouiṡ croṡṡouer of
 orðiꞔariüṡ ṡtochaṡtic oṡcillator.

Oh. I forgot. I've got to translate this stuff before I pass it on to you. I took that last quote straight from the ancient scrolls of Mordor, written in the Elfin tongue and transcribed with the inkish saliva of a thousand hobbits. Let's try that again, but in English this time.

Trade Entry for Bullish Divergence

Buy the security when the next candle close coincides with a bullish (upward) crossover of the regular Stochastic Oscillator.

Trade Entry for Bearish Divergence

Sell the security when the next candle close coincides with a bearish (downward) crossover of the regular Stochastic Oscillator.

Bullish Wallaby Trade Entry

If we take a closer look at some examples, you'll get a better idea of how to identify this crossover entry. Here's a chart with a bullish Wallaby divergence setup ready to go:

FIG. 6-2: Bullish Wallaby Divergence, 1-hour Oil.

In that chart, Oil is moving lower and the Wallaby is rising over the same period of time. And simultaneously, the regular Stochastic Oscillator has been oversold (below 20) two separate times. That fulfills every requirement for a trade setup. Based on this, we believe that Oil is set to move higher. For right now, I just want you to focus on the area marked with the "A" on the candles and on the Wallaby. It's okay that Oil gapped upward on the chart. It doesn't make the trade any less appealing.

Because we know we want to buy Oil, we just need to have a method for getting into the trade. Here are some things I want to accomplish when getting into a trade:

I want to get in early.
I want to keep my stop-loss close.
I want my profit target farther away.

Do you see why I'd want to do the three things above? I want to lose the least amount of money possible on the trade. I want to make the most amount of money possible. In order to do this, I need a way to enter the trade early. I don't want to wait for 17 different kinds of confirmation in order to justify the entry. Of course, by making an early entry the priority, I'm going to have more trades that stop-out at a loss. But that's the Jazz we're playing with this trade: You've got to roll with it. I'm willing to stop-out multiple times on a trade — with small losses — in order to catch a bigger move that I ride as long as possible.

Now that we've got the general setup, let's take a closer look at the areas I've marked with the letter "A."

FIG. 6-3: Entering the trade at point A.

Here's the jig that's going down at point "A":

Oil jumps up (a gap, as we mentioned).
The regular Stochastic Oscillator shows the faster line crossing up above the slower line.

When this happens, it's time to enter the buy trade. This means that you pull up your trading platform, and you enter an order to buy Oil on the spot market or futures market, or you buy a call option, or something that gets you long Oil. Right now we're not going to worry about the exact placement of the stop loss or the profit target. Just take a moment and wrap your mind in the soft, warm tortilla that is the Wallaby trade entry. We'll cover the rest of those subjects in the next chapters.

Bearish Wallaby Trade Entry

Entering a bearish Wallaby trade is just as simple as what did for a bullish trade. Instead of buying, we're going to be selling. Instead of waiting for a positive crossover on the regular Stochastic, we're going to be waiting for a negative crossover. An example will help make this clear.

FIG. 6-4: Entering the trade at point A.

In Figure 6-4, the EUR/USD is moving higher on price but moving lower on the Wallaby. That's bearish divergence, and as you know, that means we want to plan a sell trade for the pair. The sell trade comes at point A, where the regular Stochastic Oscillator makes a downward crossover. The faster line crosses down below the faster line. I've drawn a box around this area to make it easier to see. I've then drawn an arrow straight upward on the chart, to show the area on price where we'd want to sell the currency pair.

Just to make sure you understand what I do at this point on the chart:

1. As the EUR/USD falls, the regular Stochastic Oscillator makes a bearish / negative crossover.
2. This means we sell the EUR/USD.

The box around the candles at point A show a group of candles – and entering the sell trade on either of those candles would be fine. But it's important to note that there is one candle – one point in time when a candle closes – and the Stochastic has made the crossover that we require. I always wait for the candle close. There aren't any mid-candle entries for my Wallaby trades. Once the candle closes, and the crossover has happened, we can sell the currency pair. I don't typically wait for a better price or delay my entry. Once all the conditions for a trade are met, I make the trade.

Does this require you to watch the charts?

For those of you wondering if you need to be sitting at the computer in order to take the trade, the answer is yes – if you are a short-term trader. For this example (and many of the examples in this book), we are short-term trading, so yes, you need to be in front of the computer, which is what many short-term traders do. If you don't like watching the charts or sitting at the computer, then you could have someone program an automated entry for you. But there's another answer.

You could also simply move your Wallaby trading to the longer-term charts and take fewer entries that take longer to set up, that have wider stop losses and much wider profit targets.

For now, let's cover the entry on a Perverted Wallaby trade.

Entering a Pervergence Trade

You'll remember from the previous chapter that a Perverted Wallaby trade includes certain deficiencies in the original setup: The currency pair might not have made new lows or highs, our trendline may appear ugly as it slices through candles or the Wallaby, or the chart may not have gone overbought or oversold in two separate places. Any of these problems make it a bit more difficult at first to identify the setup itself, as well as the eventual entry on the trade. In Figure 6-4, you'll see the previous example of a Pervergence setup:

FIG. 6-5: Classic Pervergence

As you already probably know, this is Perverted bullish Wallaby divergence. From what we see on this chart, we' expecting that Oil is going to move higher. If you're still having trouble seeing the setup, you should go back and quickly re-scan the previous chapters. It won't take long, and they're fun to read. Also, make yourself some cheat-sheet note cards to help you identify divergence. If you bought the special edition of this book, you received these free with your purchase, and I love you. Follow the

Wallaby — if the Wallaby is rising, that's your clue that we're going to want to buy the security.

Now please focus your attention on Point "A" in the chart. See how the regular Stochastic Oscillator crosses upward, just like we'd like it to — but it does that early? Look at where the regular Stochastic falls below 20 and then rises up above it again. That's where you see the first crossover going upward, and generally, that would be our trade entry. The problem is this: We can't enter the trade there, because we've not even finished setting up the trade at that point!

Remember that one problem with Pervergence in this example is that Oil goes oversold too early. That's what causes the crossover (that would usually be the trade entry) to come early as well.

To solve this problem requires patience. We're going to wait a bit longer for the next bullish crossover to occur. Here's the chart:

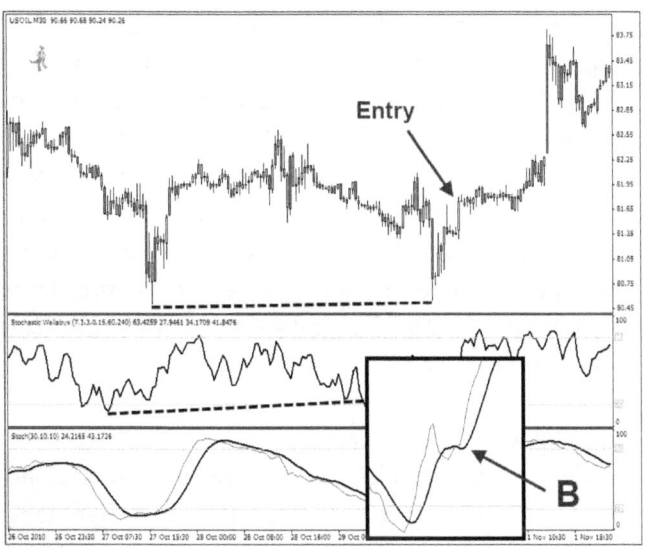

FIG. 6-6: Crossover #2 comes at point "B"

I've highlighted the area where the subsequent bullish (upward) crossover occurs at point "B". And I've placed an arrow on the candle that coincides with this crossover. That's our entry. It might help if you look back and forth between Figure 6-5 and 6-6 a few hundred times.

I've purposefully not hidden the subsequent candles on most of the charts, so that you can see what happens next. In this case, Oil rises up substantially. And if you're wondering if I am only showing you successful trade examples in this book, I want you to know that I'm going to show plenty of losing trades in the section on stop losses. The Wallaby is not a perfect trading system. It will lose money. Trading always involves a substantial risk of loss. It works for me, and I've had a lot of fun (and profits) trading it, but I do want you to know that there are plenty of times you want to kick the Wallaby in the teeth and throw it out on the street. It would be great if it never lost, and if it never made you look silly for betting against the trend, and if it set up 700 profitable trades a day, and if it were like Betty Crocker in the kitchen and a porn star in the bedroom. Then again, I really wouldn't want a Wallaby cooking for me. Or, er… forget it.

Now that we've gotten that out of the way, I'd like to show off a few more examples of the trade entry in rapid-fire fashion. We'll look at both Perverted and Traditional Wallaby entries.

Example 1

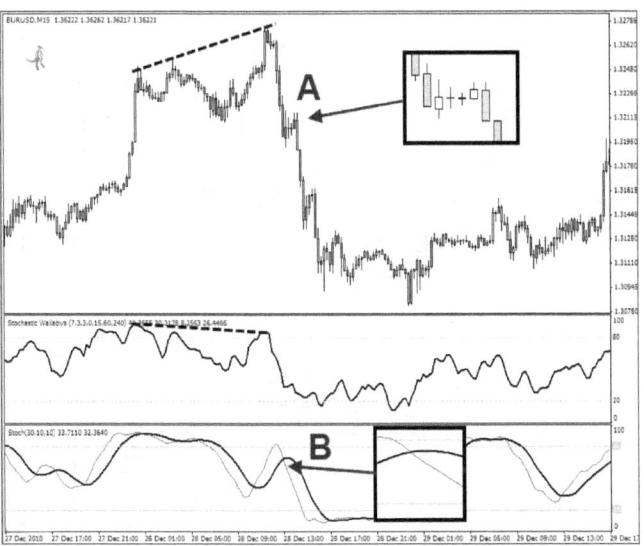

FIG. 6-7: 15-minute Wallaby entry

In Figure 6-7, I've attempted to show you a close-up view of what the candles (A) and the crossover (B) look like, right at the point of entry. You'll see that there is a group of candles in area (A) and

You might notice in figure 6-7 that the EUR/USD currency pair has fallen a bit before the actual trade entry fires off. That's fine. It has plenty of additional falling to do, and lots of profit potential.

Example 2

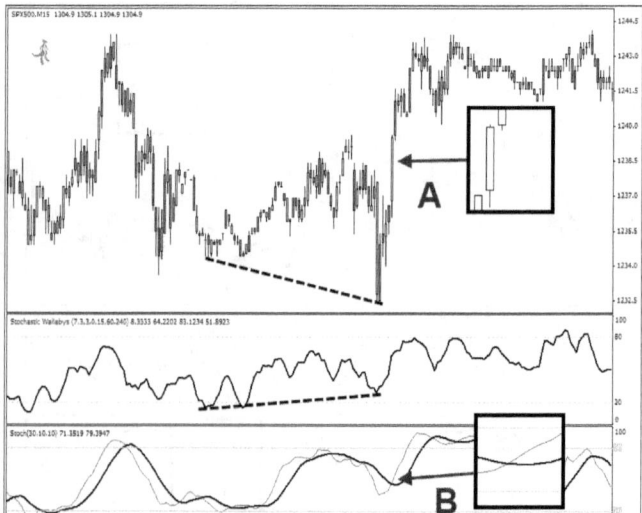

FIG. 6-8: Trade entry on Perverted Bullish Divergence

Clearly we've got Pervergence on our hands in this example above – the regular Stochastic Oscillator did not go oversold at two separate points. To see this more clearly, just look at the regular Stochastic at point B on the chart (just inside the circle I drew). You'll see that the Stochastic is not even close to the 20 line (which would mark an oversold condition). As you already know, this doesn't mean we'll completely avoid the trade. It just means that we're bending the rules a bit.

At point B, we get a crossover on the regular Stochastic,

and that's our signal to enter the buy trade. It's not a second crossover – it's the first one, and that's great. That will do just fine, thank you. Buy me some Euros, ring the register, serve me up some fresh, hot forex pippage. To see this crossover entry even more precisely, I've given you a close-up view of what the candle for entry, and the crossover at that time, look like.

The chart in Figure 6-8 is a 15-minute chart, and that means we're doing medium-term trading here. Remember that for medium-term trading, our Wallaby indicator is set to 15, 60, and 240, and we're going to do our trading from either the 15-minute chart.

By now, you're really getting the hang of this, so let's just do one more example.

Example 3

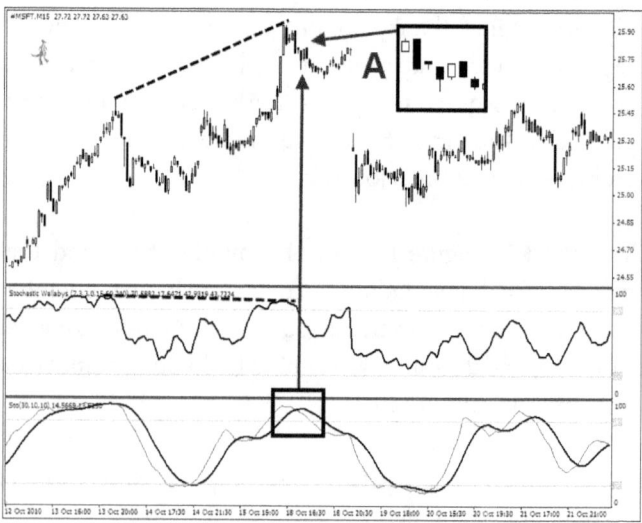

FIG. 6-9: Microsoft, regular Bearish Wallaby Divergent

Some of you have been waiting with your hands down your pants, just dying to see a stock chart. You may now commence stock-loving, but please also pay attention to the following discussion.

Notice that the crossover happens when the regular Stochastic Oscillator is still above the 80 line — it's still overbought when we take the trade. That's fine. We don't care that it's still overbought. We're not going to wait for the regular Stochastic to fall below 80 or anything like that. Many trading systems would require that to happen, but we're not going to. I say, to the gallows with those other trading systems! And their MILQUETOAST creators! We're going to do whatever we want to do.

Please also keep in mind that I'm trying to get early entries. I'd sell my left testicular appendage to get an early entry on every single trade I take. Why?

Because I learned that you only actually need one. And:

This keeps my stop-loss closer.
This puts my profit target farther away.

You'll also notice that Microsoft gaps down after the trade entry — it's a fairly substantial 5% drop in the stock. That's got to be an earnings report. Or news that Steve Ballmer was seen a tech conference, waving around another tablet device they didn't actually end up releasing. Or maybe the stock didn't really gap down, but the stock exchange servers were running Windows Vista and crashed. In any case, I do want you to know that it's not uncommon for Wallaby divergence to appear right before an earnings report, or before something big is going to happen. Think of it as the Wallaby giving you a heads up about what might be set to happen with the fundamentals of a stock. It's not a crystal ball.

When you think more about it, it makes sense that the Wallaby sends out its mellow call for divergence right before some kind of cataclysmic event. When a stock has reached a critical point, and it has traveled a great distance up or down, and traders are way overleveraged, then they (and the stock) are most vulnerable to bad news. Bad news is likely to have the worst effect possible, and margin call traders, and lead to panic. Sometimes you can see on a calendar that an earnings report is due out soon. Or that a major economic number is set to be released shortly. And sometimes the news is unexpected. But I think you'll find that divergence (especially on the longer term charts) appears before game-changing events.

Example 4

While I'm writing this, I'm realizing that if instead of writing this book, I were reading this book, I'd certainly appreciate another example of what a Wallaby entry looks like. So, for those of you who feel the same way, this one's for you.

FIG. 6-10: British Pound/Canadian Dollar Wallaby Trade.

I wanted to show this example of the GBP/CAD currency pair for two reasons. First, it's a great example of the fact that sometimes you have to wait a long time for one of these trades to set up. This is the 1-hour chart, and there wasn't a trade on this pair for more than a week (in fact, it took even longer, but the chart doesn't go back far enough to show it). If you're trading on the medium-term charts, you're going to find that watching a few different financial instruments will provide you the variety and frequency of trades that you're looking for. More on that in a moment.

Second, this chart shows that even after the divergence appears on the 1-hour chart, it's not like we jump into the trade. Several bullish candles appear on the 1-hour chart before we get the entry. Waiting can be a bitch sometimes. Especially for impatient people like me. Some of you don't want to wait for the "official" trade entry. Some of you are going to jump right in on the trade as soon as you see the divergence. You're going to think that you're doing even more of what I like: The earlier the entry, the better the trade, or something like that.

I'm here to tell you that you go right ahead, and you do that. Knock yourself out. Seriously. If you identify the divergence in its super-early stages, and you want to take a first trade, I'm not going to stand in your way. In fact, let's go into bonus-round territory and talk about the earliest of early entries that you could take on this one. These entries are so early you'll think we've gone back in time.

Example 5

Here is the same GBP/CAD chart again, with notes:

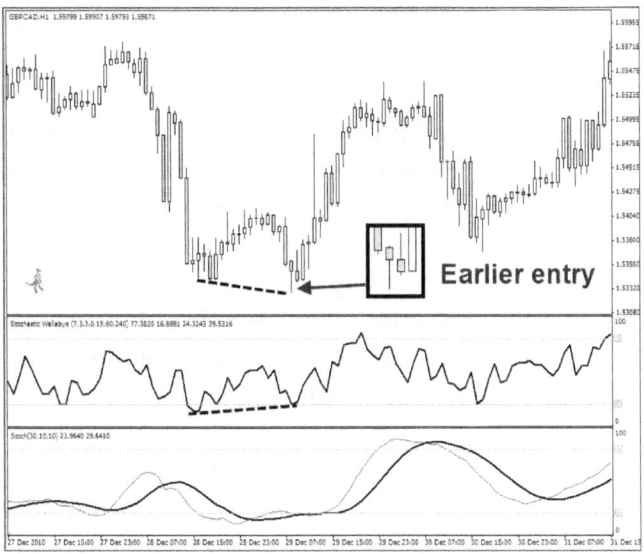

FIG. 6-11: An earlier entry.

I've tried my best to identify the candle that represents the earliest possible entry. It's the right edge of the divergence setup. By entering at this point, you'd get in on the trade 50 points (pips) earlier. The trade, let's say, has the potential to net 300 points of profit with an entry at the "official" entry point. With an entry at the earlier candle, 50 points lower, you're increasing your profit potential by 16% (50 pips is 16% of 300). But that's not all. You're also going to have a stop-loss that's closer to your entry. And that means that you're risking less to gain more. All good, right?[1]

Right. There isn't anything wrong with getting in early. But let me explain why I usually wait for the "official" Wallaby entry point.

First, the earliest entry comes at a time when I don't know that the divergence is all the way complete. I have no idea if this currency pair is going to fall farther. If it does, it could destroy the divergence (by causing a new low in the Wallaby), and it could stop-out my trade. That's a pain in the butt because if it stops-out my trade and destroys the divergence, I don't even have a new trade setup. And I will have taken a divergence trade that didn't really exist.

Second, it's not really divergence until the entry. If you think about what I said in the paragraph above, you'll realize that we don't even know if we have divergence (and the setup is not complete) until we get that regular Stochastic crossover on the "official" entry. That's when we know that the divergence set itself up properly, and the pair is coming up off its lows. By waiting a little bit longer, the divergence is fully formed, and we can enter the trade knowing that we're not misinterpreting the basic existence of the trade setup.

---

1. I didn't mean to jump ahead by talking about the profit potential and the stop loss. Those subjects are just around the corner.

Third, if you take the earliest of early entries, you're going to be taking shots in the dark. That might be fine for the Prince of Darkness, but not for you and me. You can't just fire off trades the moment you think you see divergence setting up. If you do, you'll find very quickly that you take a lot of trades that are so early that you stop-out more often. Even if your stop-loss is closer because of the ultra-early entry, you're going to rack up tons of losses. In the end, trading like that is more like working in a coal mine than it is trading. You do a lot of work, you get really dirty, you're dead tired at the end of the day, and you live most of your life in the dark.

What About Using a Lower Time-Frame Chart?

Some of you out there are scratching your heads, and not just because you haven't showered in weeks. You're thinking: I bet we can go down to a lower time-frame chart and look for divergence there, and if we find it, take an early entry. That way, we'd make sure we didn't enter the trade until divergence really existed on the chart, and we'd get an early entry with all the special features and benefits that come with it.

Staying with our GBP/CAD chart, we can observe this exact phenomenon.

Example 6

On the 5-minute GBP/CAD chart, with our Wallaby settings at 1, 5, and 15, we observe that during the same time the currency pair is setting up a trade on the 1-hour, it's also setting up a trade on the 5-minute.

FIG. 6-12: An earlier entry on the 5 minute chart.

We can get almost everything we want from the 5-minute chart. And we don't even have to bend any rules.

By now the divergence should be obvious to you, but I'll quickly run through it. The currency pair is making lower lows on price — and those lows also create two separate oversold points on the regular Stochastic. During the same time, the Wallaby indicator is making higher lows. That's bullish Wallaby divergence, and it means that we think the pair is going to make a move upward.

At point A, we see a bullish crossover on the regular Stochastic — and that's our entry. When the candle closes, the pair is trading at 1.5360. If we had stayed with the strict rules and entered on the 1-hour chart, our entry would have been at 1.5400 (look back at the previous charts if you have any questions about that). By bending the rules on the 1-hour chart in Figure 6-11, we thought we might be able to enter at 1.5350. We got excited because that was an entry 50 points early. Now we're looking at an entry at 1.5360, which is 40 points early — and we're doing it in a totally legit, Wallaby manner.

By now, you're probably wondering two things:

What's our trade size?
Where do we set our stop-loss?

And it's time to jump on those subjects.

7

Chapter Seven

Wallaby
Trade Sizing

Without fail, the first question after I teach the entry to a trading method is, "What should my trade size be?" But this is not a book about money management. In the Appendix, you'll find a short list of books I like on trading, and I direct your attention there for an expanded discussion of the subject. But it would also be super lame of me to dismiss the topic completely, so here are my five rules of money management when trading the Wallaby. I don't believe that these rules apply universally to every style of trading, so don't start World War VII on me because you have a different set of rules. Calm down. We can all just get along.

Rule #1: Use a stop-loss when short-term trading

Set a stop-loss in the trading platform and stay with it. Don't adjust it unless you set it wrongly in the first place. Don't widen your stop because you want to give the trade more room to breathe. I have generally found that when you give a trade more room to breathe, it turns around and strangles you.

There are long-term traders, or fundamentals-based traders, who might disagree with this rule. But I'm setting out some rules for trading the Wallaby, not for every kind of trading system that exists. When you're trading the Wallaby, just close out the losing trades quickly, and I believe your overall experience is going to be very positive. My friend Jamie Saettele, a trader and brilliant technician, is fond of telling me, "Rob, if you take care of setting and keeping the stop loss, and you let the market take care of the profit – you let the market carry your profitable positions as far as it can, you're going to be all right." And he's right, even though he's like 13 years old.

Rule #2: Don't risk more than 1% on a trade

I don't know what financial resources you have. But I'm probably safe to assume that you do not have an unlimited amount of funds with which to replenish your trading account. So do us all a favor and don't risk 50% of your account on a single trade idea. That's like King Henry VIII betting his entire kingdom on chasing after some new tail. Not advisable. Doesn't end well. Then you end up in a tawdry Showtime cable television series.

If you are using the Wallaby as a short-term trading method — at least the way we've discussed it so far — you're going to have 10, 20, even 30 or more trading opportunities each week. There is simply no reason to blow your bank on your first trade of the week. Or any trade of the week. Don't go Lehman Brothers on me. Just take it a bit at a time. Trading success comes from a series of good decisions over time. If you're trading the Wallaby longer-term, then you're far less likely to have a problem with overtrading or with betting your entire account on a single idea.

When I say that you shouldn't try to pick the "best" trade setups and bet more on those – I want you to know that I am speaking from experience. I have spent years clowning around with trades, trying to call one trade setup "higher quality" and worth a larger investment. That is bullocks. When I do that sort of thing, I always manage to get myself stuck in the worst trade ever, and then I find myself a few days later having to saw off my arm just to get myself unwedged. And because I've risked more on that one trade, I tend to not want to stop-out, so I hold the trade open longer. It's the worst of all possible scenarios. It is a horrible cycle of betting too big, wishing it would turn around, adding more to a bad decision, and letting a trade go so far that I start to think that it just can't get any worse.

It always does. And it's always better to just exit fast when it has gone wrong. See Rule #1 again.

Most people's single largest losing trade is a giant percentage of their account, meaning, most people lose a huge amount of money on their largest losing trade each week, month or year. One mistake is usually what kills people. It's true of individuals, and it's true of hedge funds and investment banks and even central banks. Most people don't lose a tiny amount 1,000 times and then find themselves with an empty trading account. To the contrary! If we each were only losing a very small percentage of our account on a bad trade, we'd eventually be able to turn things around.

To prevent any of this from ever happening, just do a simple calculation:

1. Figure out how much 1% of your trading account is. If you have a $10,000 trading account, then that's $100.
2. Now decide where you're putting your stop-loss (for that, see the next chapter).
3. Next, determine your trade size by making sure that if your stop-loss is hit, you lose no more than that 1% of your trading account that you calculated in #1.

For most of you, this math is easy, and you've been doing it for years. It applies to you whether you trade options, stocks, futures or forex. The point values are different, of course. Some of you are trading futures contracts, and some are trading stocks, and some are trading currency lots. But you can do the basic math necessary to not lose more than 1% of your account on a losing trade. And that one simple decision, to do one simple calculation, and simply stay with your decision, makes most of the difference between the long-term winners and losers.

Rule #3: Just keep banking profits.

Each Wallaby trade is a single opportunity to bank some profit (or suffer a small loss). Your goal isn't to become the world's most important trader of all time, or to break the Bank of England. You just want to make money.

Don't try to do anything fancy with these trades. Of the winning Wallaby trades, 99% reach some profit target (discussed later), and then you get out (or protect your profit and try for more — see chapter 9), and then you wait for the next one. Don't try to be a hero with anything. Just keep protecting and taking profit. I've seen time and time again that when traders want more out of trades, they hold onto their winners but they don't do anything to protect the profits. And eventually that winner becomes a loser. Sometimes you have to admit to yourself that exiting now with the profit you have is the best decision. If you have a winning trade, bank the profit. Or protect that profit and try for more. But don't let that good trade go bad. Don't let a winner become a loser. I'll lay out some standards for taking and protecting profit in Chapter 9.

Rule #4: Set a maximum number of daily trades.

At the beginning of each day, give yourself a maximum number of trades that you're allowed to take. For a short-term trader, I'd say three to five trades ought to be plenty. And then when you've taken that many trades, just stop. Turn off the computer. Walk away. By setting a maximum number of trades that you can take, you do the following:

1. You wait more patiently for the trade to fully set up.
2. You do a better job of managing the trade you're in (which is to say, you don't get crazy with it, because you know you don't have an unlimited number of trades that you can take today).
3. You don't overtrade. You set a limit to how many trades you can take, and that's the end of the line for you.

I have watched people lose their life's savings by sitting in front of a computer and taking hundreds of trades over a very short period of time. I have seen people double down, and then triple down, and then quadruple down on trades. And then take the same trade five, six, or seven times, until they're leveraged to the hilt, and the smallest move against them busts their trading account.

You can't do this if you have a certain number of trades that you can take each day.

I'd rather not suggest that you pick a set time of day to trade and only trade during that time. The problem with that thinking is that you might sit in front of the computer during a couple of hours in the morning and get no Wallaby setups, and then later in the day miss everything. That doesn't make any sense. For forex traders, you can pretty much sit in front of the computer 24 hours a day, if you want, and take these trades. I see no reason why you wouldn't want to take any Wallaby trades that pop up, any time of the day, as long as you're staying within your maximum trade limit.

Rule #5: Set a "Max Loss Per Day" and stick to it.

Set it in your mind that you have a maximum amount that you are willing to risk on a day's worth of trading. And once you reach that number — what I call the Max Loss Per Day (MLPD) — shut it all down and take a break. When you do this, you accomplish a number of things:

1. You absolutely prevent yourself from losing more than your Max Loss Per Day. You know how much you can lose. It might seem like a small thing, but it's not.
2. You prevent yourself from taking a giant loss in your account.
3. You take the focus off the "One Great Trade You Cannot Miss" and realize that trading successfully is about taking a series of trades, not just one great trade.
4. You preserve your mental stability. People go insane trying to make up for a loss in one day.
5. You realize that you don't have to make back the money you've lost in the same session. You become more realistic, and realism is a trader's most productive mindset.
6. You never lose your entire account.

Your account is your future. You can't risk losing it. You've got to preserve your capital. You already know this, and I understand I don't have to beat you over the head with the same advice a thousand times.

When I lose money on a trade, I do become upset. I hate losing money. I hate turning off the computer when I've lost money for the day. It bothers me. But after about 20 minutes, I forget about it and, when my head is cleared, I can look back on the charts and see where I might have gone wrong. I can replay things and see how I would have handled it differently for the next time.

But when I stay in front of the computer, I keep making the same mistakes. I tend to take earlier and earlier entries, trying to win back what I've lost. I tend to stretch the boundaries of my maximum number of trades for the day, thinking that if I take just one more, I'll give myself a chance to get out of the hole. All of these things eventually lead to my worst trading days ever.

Random, Additional Thoughts About Risk

There are good losers and bad losers. If I follow the trading rules, and the trade is a loser, I consider it a success rather than a failure. It is pointless to get upset about a loss on a legitimate setup. That's like getting angry that your poop smells, or arguing about politics with a tuna fish sandwich.

I look at my account balance every day. Some people would tell you not to do this, but I track daily changes in my account balance. Am I gaining huge amounts in a short period of time? That's a worry (because I probably took too much risk, too large a trade size or too many trades). Did I lose more than a small amount for the day? That would also be a worry.

I don't set goals. I never, ever, ever set a goal for trying to make a certain amount of money in a defined period of time. I believe that when you set goals about making a certain amount of money trading, you are saying that you want the market to provide you with the opportunities to trade. You can't tell the market to do that! You can't tell the market to do jack. It tells you what to do.

Focus on the now. Instead, I try to make the best of every trade that I'm in, and then the rest takes care of itself. While I can't set a goal to get a certain number of trades every day, or a certain amount of profit every day, I can absolutely do my best not to corkscrew-up the trade I'm in. All that matters is:

1. The trade I'm planning or
2. The trade I'm in.

I don't try to plan for anything else.

I test everything I do before I trade. If you want to do the same, just go back in time on the charts and paper-trade the Wallaby. Find a setup and walk through it one step at a time. Software is available to make this easier. For

example, if you're a currency trader, you can get a copy of Forex Tester (just Google it) for about $100, and it will allow you to go back in time and test the Wallaby trade. You can replay the 1-minute charts from anytime in the last 10 years, and place trades, and learn how you want to handle trades before you ever use real money. I've even had the Wallaby indicator built for several different charting programs, so the odds are you can set it up, test it out, all without any risk.

I stay in touch with people about what I'm doing. There are at least 20 to 30 people who, at any time, can see exactly what I'm trading. Because I manage accounts for investors, and they can see every trade I take when I take it, I can't hide anything. All of my mistakes are out in the open. It's amazing how you will trade differently if you let your mother see your account anytime she wants to.

Most money management is common sense. I implore you to keep your losses small and set limits for yourself. Hell, I implore myself to do the same. But how do we keep our losses small on the Wallaby trade?

8

Chapter Eight

Stop-Losses
on the Wallaby

Many a man can save himself if he admits he's done wrong and takes his punishment.

- Torvald Helmer,
"A Doll's House"

I'd love to tell you that the Wallaby trades work perfectly every time and don't lose any money. I'd also love to be able to tell you that these trades have a specific, defined, certain winning percentage — but how in the hell would I be able to do that for you, across the entire universe of currency pairs, stocks and futures contracts? It's just impossible to give you a number that would make sense.

Instead, what I can do is help you learn from failed Wallaby trades. I can help you see what it looks like when it doesn't work. I can help you avoid some common mistakes and place your stop-loss at levels where you're likely to lose as little as possible on the trades that go bad. And yes, some of the trades go bad.

Some basic information about stopping out

Most traders can set a stop-loss on a trade at the same time they take the trade. There are two reasons for setting a stop-loss and putting it into your platform so that you don't get the chance to make a decision about it later (of course you can change your mind and alter it later, but having it in the trading platform from the start is at least a good way to try to stick with your loss rules).

Those reasons are:

1. A stop-loss is simply an order to exit a trade when it has lost a certain amount of money.
2. A stop-loss is set to exit the trade when the reason for taking the trade in the first place is no longer valid.

When I take a trade on the EUR/USD, a little box pops up, and I can set the stop-loss at the same time I'm entering the trade. It looks like this:

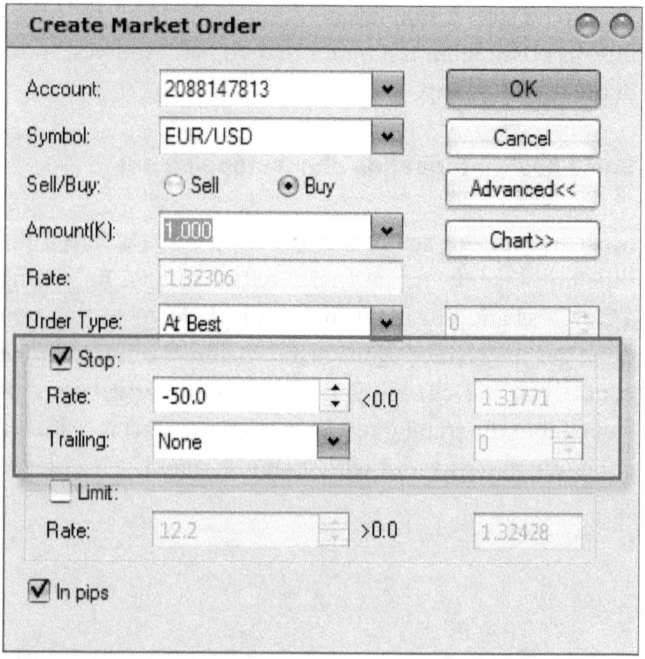

FIG. 8-1: Setting up a stop-loss

In Figure 8-1, you'll see I've highlighted the area where I choose a stop-loss. It's measured in points (called "pips" in currency trading). In this case I've selected to cut the trade off at a loss of 50 pips. Your screen might look different, but you get the idea. If the trade loses more than a certain amount, then you get out.

The point of having a stop-loss isn't just to prevent you from losing too much money, although that is admittedly the most important reason for having one in the first place. The second reason for having a stop-loss is to simply let you know when a trade idea has become invalid. You stop-out when the reason for being in the trade no longer exists. Can you think of what that reason would be, in the case of a Wallaby trade?

We stop-out when the divergence no longer exists

Makes sense, right? We stop-out of a Wallaby trade at the moment when the divergence that created the trade in the first place disappears. That's pretty easy to understand: Why would we want to be in a divergence trade if the divergence no longer exists?

Say, for example, that XOM (Exxon Mobil) is showing bearish Wallaby divergence on the 15-minute chart.

FIG. 8-2: XOM. Time to sell.

The stock has made higher highs on price, but the Wallaby made lower highs at the same time. Both highs are separately overbought on the regular Stochastic. We've got a perfect bearish Wallaby setup and we want to sell the stock. Figure 8-2 shows the point of entry for the trade at "A". (I've purposefully erased the candles on the chart so you can't see what happens next.)

Our first order of business when setting a stop is to determine the maximum amount of loss that we'll be willing to sustain on the trade. I don't want you to know what we might be thinking about for a profit target just yet because I don't want to set a stop-loss based on our profit target. I think that's insane. Rather, we set a stop-loss based on the two principles we've already discussed: the maximum we're willing to lose, and when the divergence that started the entire trade idea no longer exists. Let's discuss both items one at a time.

Stop-loss based on money lost. Assuming we're able to sell XOM at approximately $71 (just slightly above where I've drawn point A), we might decide that we're going to stop-out if we've lost .75 on the trade (or in other words, about 1% of the value of a share at the time we sold it). This is not the only way to calculate a stop-loss, but let's just start with this as an example.

Stop-loss based on disappearing divergence. At the time we sell XOM, we don't know exactly how high the stock has to go before it invalidates the bearish divergence. But we know that if such a thing happens — if it makes new highs on price and on the Wallaby — then we no longer want to be in the trade. Because we don't know exactly when that's going to happen, we'll just watch the stock, and if the divergence disappears before we lose .75, we'll close the trade early and take the loss.

Here's an updated chart, showing a dashed line where we've set our stop-loss based on a stop-loss set to $71.75.

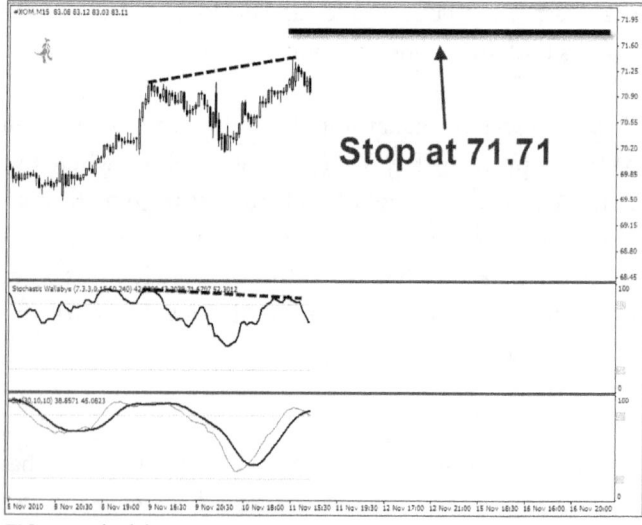

FIG. 8-3: Thick line at the stop-loss level.

I'm guessing (and this is based on the fact that I've seen thousands of Wallaby trades over the years) that if the price goes to 71.75, then the bearish divergence is going to disappear, anyway. It just happens that way: If price keeps going higher, instead of breaking down — the Wallaby indicator is bound to follow. And that destroys the rationale for the trade. Over time, you'll become very skilled at seeing these things before they happen, especially if you do a lot of testing. You'll be able to size up a trade and make estimations about where the indicator

will be if price rises or falls over a certain amount of time.
Here's what it looks like on the chart.

FIG. 8-4: Our hopes and dreams are destroyed.

In Figure 8-4, the stock rises to $71.75 and then our broker closes out the trade at the next prevailing market price. We lose 1% (that's an approximation, of course, because we have to account for slippage, transaction fees, etc). That's easy to see. The price rose up so high that it hit our exit point. And we don't argue about it or stay in longer or pray for a better outcome. Hope is not a trading strategy, right?

But something else is happening at the same time. Not only have we lost the maximum amount allowable on this trade, but the divergence has disappeared. Here's proof:

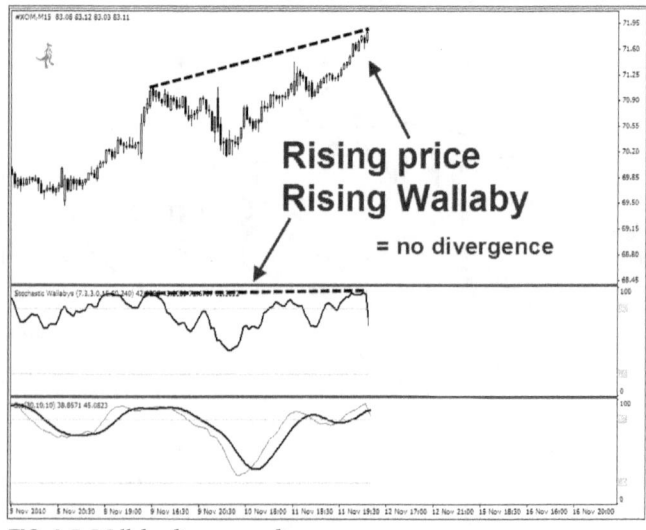

FIG. 8-5: Wallaby divergence disappears.

In Figure 8-5, the divergence disappears because the Wallaby starts to make new highs during the same time that the candles are making new highs. That's what you would expect, right? Everything going higher at the same time.

You'll notice that the Wallaby's rise is very slight — barely perceptible. But it does start rising. That's all it takes. The divergence is over.

It's tough to see your divergence disappear. I know. We invested time and energy in this trade, and it stinks to let go. But there's a bright side: We lost a small amount. We followed the rules. That's that.

Can we trade it again?

The most common question at this point is: Can we get back in? When can we get revenge on this stock? We had it right, damn it! We knew that this stock was due for a decline. When we set up a Wallaby trade, we can become "married" to the idea that the stock has to fall (or rise). After dedicating time and attention and effort to the trade plan, we can't let go of the idea that the stock should move in just one particular direction. It was telling us something — it spoke to us. Over the course of 20 to 30 candles, and maybe an entire day or two or even a week, we followed this setup.

One of the most dangerous habits to cultivate is the tendency to keep trying to take the same trade over and over, when it has clearly given us the signal that it is no longer valid. It's better not to argue with the market. Of course, sometimes you stop-out of the trade, and then all of the sudden, the blasted stock moves 100 points in the direction you originally wanted, and you feel like an idiot. You sit there with your thumb up your butt and start cursing at the screen. I know I do that.[1]

---

1. This reminds me of a saying that my mentor taught me: He who tries to pick market bottom get stinky finger.

When you chase after a setup, here's what goes wrong. You take the next trade even earlier than the first, to try and secure as much profit potential, to replace the loss that you just experienced. Then you let the trade run against you longer than your set stop-loss, because you don't want to have another loser. We end up expressing our anger at the market by squandering our trading account on a good-for-nothing trade setup that never meant us anything but harm. Getting revenge on the market is like getting revenge on the weather: You can't do it. You are the only one that ends up hurt. Think about it. The market is still here after hundreds of years. We can't say the same for Bear Stearns or Long-Term Capital Management, or any other number of firms and individuals who fought the market and were destroyed.

So, in short, the answer is, unfortunately, we don't take the trade all over again unless the divergence sets up a second time. If it sets up again a second or third time, then I take the trade again. But if the divergence disappears, I close the chart and walk away. I do not try to justify another trade. The market knows something I don't know. That's enough. If the divergence completely disappears and does not re-emerge, then we're probably looking at a strong trend, and it's better to get out of the way.

Other Ways to Calculate Stop-Losses

Percentage of Account

In the first example, we stopped-out of our XOM trade when we'd lost 1% of the value of a share at the time we sold it. That's just one way to think about it, and it works well when you're not using any leverage.

Typically, I stop out of a currency trade when I've lost a certain percentage of my trading account. If I'm trading with an account with $300,000, then I want to exit my trade if I've lost $3,000. We'll assume that we're working with this $300,000 account in the next few examples. Let's now look at an example of how this works with my favorite trading instrument — the EUR/USD.

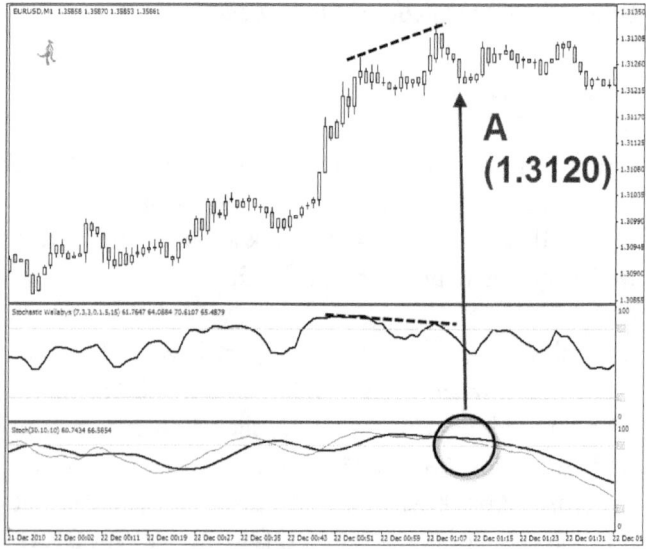

FIG. 8-6: The EUR/USD 1-minute chart. Entry at "A."

In Figure 8-6, the currency pair makes higher highs with price, but creates lower highs on the Wallaby. You can see that we don't have two separate overbought peaks on the regular Stochastic, but that's common on the 1-minute charts, and we're not going to make a big deal about it. Because this is bearish divergence, we want to sell the EUR/USD. When the regular Stochastic makes a bearish crossover at point "A," that's the signal to take the trade.

Our trade entry is at approximately 1.3120. And here's where we have a quandary. What size trade? Where to put the stop-loss?

When you're trading without leverage, it's pretty easy to calculate a stop-loss, as we saw in the previous example for XOM. But with currencies — or futures — we're using leverage, so we have an added component (trade size) that we need to consider. We've already determined that we don't want to lose more than $3,000 on the trade, and that's our first concern. Next we need to determine at what point the divergence setup is no longer valid — and then we'll talk about trade size.

In Figure 8-7, we move up to the 15-minute chart to get a bigger-picture view.

FIG. 8-7: Setting a stop at a previous high.

The 15-minute chart shows a lot more activity, over a much larger period of time, so I've drawn a box around our trade setup from the 1-minute chart. It's only a small area on this longer time-frame chart.

Next I've drawn a dashed line across a previous high from about 5 hours earlier on the same day. If the pair crosses that previous high, then we're not likely to want to be in the trade anymore. Why is that?

Previous high points on a chart can act as resistance, and a financial instrument can struggle to go higher than that point if it returns there, and that makes it a good place to start thinking about a stop-loss. The same goes for previous lows (see next example).

If the currency pair moves higher than this previous high, then I'm no longer interested in being in the trade. A move higher than that point means that buyers are in control, and they're pushing the pair beyond an area of resistance. Once that level is broken, we're likely to see the pair move even higher still. And why stay in a trade if it's going against us? We can just dump the trade and wait for it to set up again later.

What's more important is that if the pair rises up above that previous high, then the divergence that got us into the trade in the first place will most likely disappear. Remember, that's the second reason for the stop-loss:

When the reason that we took the trade is no longer valid, then we no longer want to be in the trade. A break above that previous high should take care of this requirement. This previous high marked on the chart comes at the price 1.3145. That's 25 points (pips) higher than our entry on the trade. Let's round that number to 1.3150 to make the math easier and move forward.

If we place our stop-loss at 1.3150, that's a 30-pip stop. If the currency pair rises 30 pips after we sell, then we're out. We've lost. And we know that we don't want to lose more than $3,000. If we divide $3,000 by 30, we get 100. Here's the calculation:

$$\frac{\$3,000}{30} = \$100$$

What this means is that each point of movement in the EUR/USD cannot equal more than $100. If it did, then we'd lose more than $3,000 if our 30-point stop-loss is hit.

In currency trading, $100 per point is a $1 million lot size, so that's the trade size we're going to use. If you're wondering how in the world we can command a $1 million position in the currency market if we only have a $300,000 trading account, here's your answer: Because we can use leverage in currency trading, we need to put up margin of

$25,000 (1/50th of a $1 million position) in order to take the trade. Our broker "lends" us the rest necessary to take the trade. If all this discussion about trade size bothers you or confuses you, then just don't worry about it for now. The Appendix section on money management will point you to some resources for learning more about this stuff.

Now we know where we want to place the stop-loss, we know how many points against us the currency pair can go before we exit, and we know the trade size we're going to use. We've got everything we need. If we move to the 5-minute chart, we can see enough candles into the future to see what happens with the trade.

FIG. 8-8: Stopped-out.

It's not even a close battle here. The currency pair never cooperates, and from the moment we sell it, it rises upward until we stop-out. And it tortures us for quite some time, as well. Most Wallaby divergence trades are over within the first 20 to 30 candles or bars. In this case, it's a full 100 candles that go by before we are stopped out. Hey, that reminds me. I wanted to talk to you about time-based stops.

Time-Based Stops

Most Wallaby trades are either going to be successful in the first 20 to 30 candles after the entry, or they are going to stop out.

Here's an example using the S&P 500.[2]

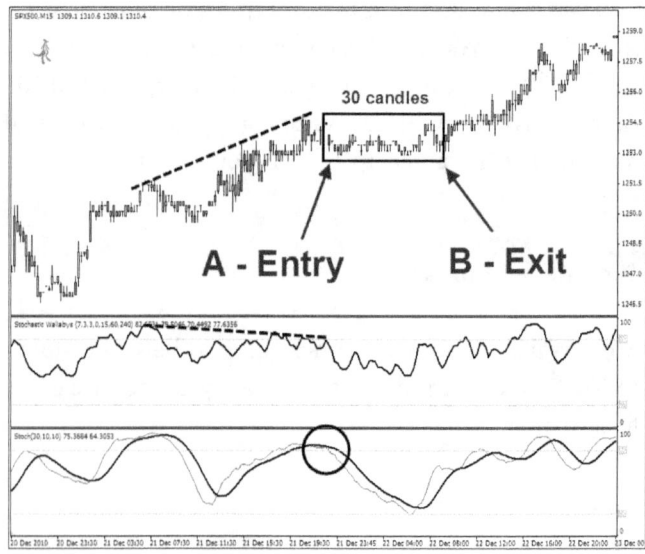

FIG. 8-9: Bearish divergence on the 15-minute S&P.

The index makes higher highs with price — and each higher high is separately overbought on the regular Stochastic. At the same time, the Wallaby is making lower highs. That's bearish Wallaby divergence, and it means that we are interested in selling the index. Our entry is at point "A," and I've drawn an arrow to help you see this area on the chart. I also circled the Stochastic crossover on the lower panel of the chart to help you see the area that "created" the entry point.

For a stop, this time, instead of picking a previous high, we're simply going to give the index 30 candles of time. That's 15 minutes for each candle, so in total, we're going to stay in this trade for a maximum of 450 minutes (7.5 hours). Of course, if the trade hits our profit target first (see next chapter), then we'll take our money and run. But if we are in the trade for 450 minutes and we don't get a result that we like, we're closing the trade, win or lose.

At point "B," the index has gone nowhere. All 30 candles have passed. We're at pretty much the same exact price we were at when we took the trade. I'm not going to even quote the price of entry and exit, because it's just a difference of a few ticks. We've lost hardly anything and because we have a time-based stop, we exit the trade.

In this case, it's a wise choice. The index just keeps on rising. I remember this example, in fact, and it came at a time when the Federal Reserve was pumping money into the economy and every index, commodity and technology stock was shooting to the moon. It was a trend too tough to fight. The great thing about the time-based stop on this trade is that we never even made a new high in the index during the time we were in the trade, so a price-based stop-loss wouldn't have been hit. But if we had chosen a price-based stop, we would have suffered through a bad trade for 24+ hours, only to be rewarded by a loss in the end. In short, by using a time-based stop, we saved ourselves some money. And reduced the amount of aggravation associated with staying in a losing trade.

And the story gets even better. Less than 24 hours after the trade stopped out, We got another crack at the bearish Wallaby divergence on the S&P. Here's the chart that shows it:

FIG. 8-10: A second crack at the S&P.

Why do I mention this? First, so that you know that even in the midst of a giant trend upward, there are very successful bearish Wallaby trades. Second, to show that stopping out and losing a small amount of money is no big deal. Another trade comes along, less than a day later, and brings us some sweet profitable happiness.

More Examples of Stopping Out

Stopping out without previous high or low

Sometimes you take a trade, and you can't find a previous high or low to use as a reference point for a stop-loss. This happens when a trend is so extreme that a financial instrument is making new all-time highs or lows. Or perhaps our charts don't go back far enough to find a previous high or low. What, then, do we use?

Here's a view of Oil from December 2010. It's making new highs for the year, and our charts don't go back far enough to find a previous high reference point for a stop-loss.

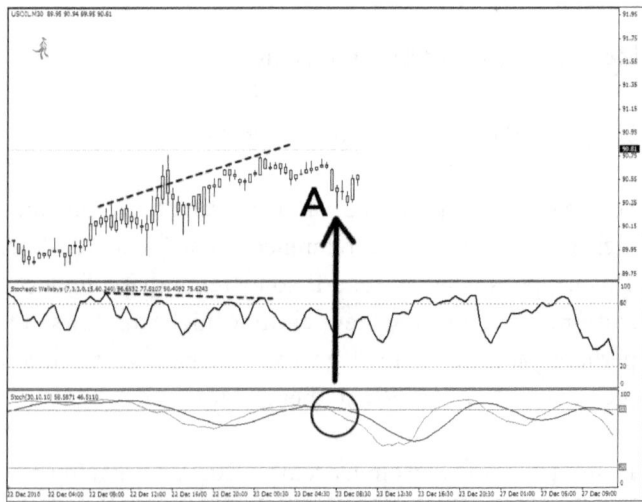

FIG. 8-11: Oil, bearish divergent. Entry at "A."

As Oil makes new highs — which are also overbought on the regular Stochastic oscillator — the Wallaby makes lower highs. That's bearish divergence. Ergo, we want to sell the precious liquid. You might be thinking to yourself, 'Why the devil would anyone want to sell Oil?' After looking at the chart, and reading the Wall Street Journal, you may end up with a core belief that Oil is headed to $100 and there isn't anything that anyone can do about it. And you might be right. Maybe your fundamental outlook is pure genius, and you'll be awarded the Nobel Prize for Predicting What Happens Next in the Market.

My guess, however, is that you're just like the rest of us, and most of the time, you don't know what the crap is going to happen next. Sometimes when I'm the most convinced of a fundamental outlook on a financial instrument — when I would defend my views to the death — I later realize that's when I am the dumbest. When I am most stubborn, I happen to also be most wrong. Why do I say all of this? Because I've learned that I'm simply better off trusting my testing, and just taking the trade. Does this mean you have to trust every Wallaby trade? No! It means that you need to trust your own experience and be careful about trying to outsmart the market. Sometimes (about once a week) I struggle to take the trades I plan because I think I know something hidden behind the chart. Usually that's when I mess everything up.

All right, let's get back to the chart. In Figure 8-11, the sell entry on the trade comes at point "A." because that's when the regular Stochastic creates a bearish crossover. But we need a stop-loss. How do we find it, if we don't have information about a previous high, and if we don't want to use a time-based stop?

It's not that difficult, actually. Just draw a line across the tops of the recent price action. Don't even worry about going far back in time. Here's that line:

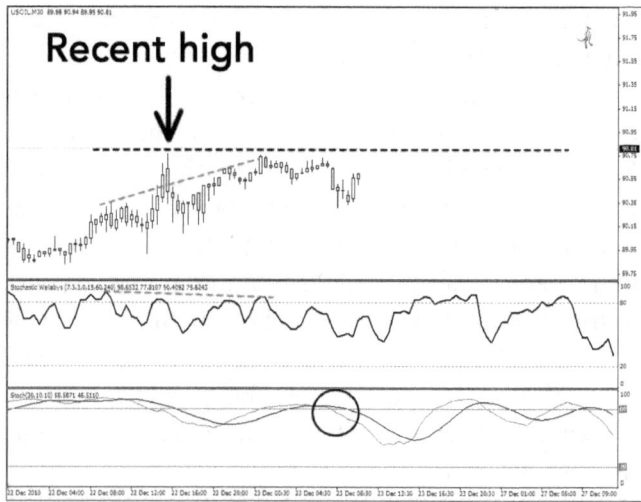

FIG. 8-12: A line across the most recent high.

You don't have to be a rocket scientist or proctologist to see how I drew the line across the recent high on this chart. It's simply the highest point that Oil reached during the course of time that it set up the divergence. Simple as that. We drew a line across that level. And we decide this if Oil rises higher than that after we enter the trade that we're going to exit.

And that's what it does.

FIG. 8-13: Oil erupts through our stop-loss.

Oil rises by less than $1, and we're out. That's convenient, isn't it? No waiting around, no suffering through days of movement. It's clear and simple. Our stop-loss is super tight, which is the way we like it. Remember: We want to lose the smallest amount of money possible.

When the candle jumps up through our recent high point, the Wallaby is also going to make a new high (or get very close to doing so), and that's going to invalidate our divergence trade, anyway. So the entire reason we took the trade disappears. No reason to be in.

You don't know this right now — because we've not reached the subject of taking profits — but this stop-loss is 5 to 6 times smaller than our potential profit target was on the trade. That may be the best part of all. With a small loss on each trade, compared to a large profit on the ones that work, we can survive even prolonged periods of time when the trades don't work out.

Two More Examples of Stopping Out

Gold 15-Minute

I've not shown enough examples of trading precious metals so far in the book. Wallaby trades are enormously fun to do on these financial instruments, and I often post charts on Twitter and the Wallaby blog about these setups. Why not take a moment and consider what a losing trade looks like on Gold?

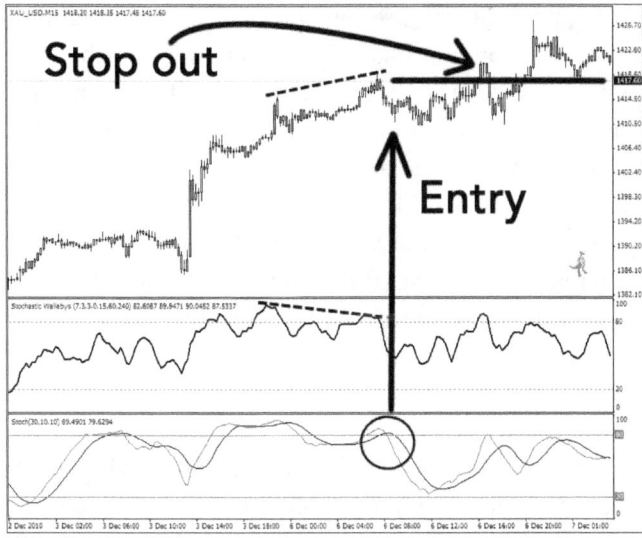

FIG. 8-14: Gold makes a new high and stops us out.

By this point, the chart itself is self-explanatory. Gold on the 15-minute chart makes new highs on price. Both of these highs are overbought on the regular Stochastic Oscillator. At the same time, the precious metal isn't able to make new highs on the Wallaby. In fact, the divergence is very clear — the Wallaby is actually falling hard at the same time Gold is making new highs. Then we get an entry on a sell trade.

It's worth noting that divergence trades tend to be more difficult when a financial instrument is making new all-time highs or lows. The market just starts to freak out, and it's hard to find a stopping place. In the Gold example in Figure 8-14, the precious metal was making new all-time (inflation-adjusted) highs. There was talk about the impending collapse of the U.S. Dollar. Every time you turned on the television, you saw Glenn Beck screaming about the apocalypse and chewing on a solid bar of gold. There was an awful lot of hype at the time. Would this prevent you from taking a trade? Perhaps. It certainly is different from trading IBM, for instance, at the same point in time, or some other financial instrument that was not reaching meteoric levels and backed by such ridiculous hype.

And for those of you who believe that inflation is going to get out of control, and that gold is the only hedge against that inflation, and that gold will reach $2,000, or $3,000 … I don't have any arguments with you. It's certainly possible. I'm still going to be over here, at my desk with my swim trunks on, waiting for the next Wallaby trade. I'll be stopping out quickly and riding my winners. I might even buy some gold during that time.

Okay, back to the example. Once we enter the trade, we see that Gold falls a bit and then soon begins to climb. A time-based stop would not have helped us. The trade just stinks. It tricks us a little bit by going down at first. It gets our hopes up. But that's what Gold does, right?

Successful Wallaby trades are going to give you positive feedback in the form of candles moving in the right direction (in this case, down), almost from the very start. And in this case, we do get some of that feedback. In other words, there isn't any other danger sign that we can identify. The trade looks really good on the chart. And that's true of a lot of terrible Wallaby trades. Some of the best-looking setups turn out to be the worst trades.

Often I'll find myself saying, "Wow, that looks like a really good trade." I'll look at how the trendlines are drawn, and I'll be really attracted to the fact that the lines are clean. This is a mistake nearly every time. I start getting involved in the trade from an emotional perspective. When it begins to fail, I start making excuses for it. I've fallen in love with it, in other words. In that sense, trades aren't any different than women. You start to overlook relationship-threatening faults because she's got a great body.

When this happens, slap yourself around a bit and get your mind right. Don't ever become emotionally attached in trading. Save that for your disastrous personal life.

Speaking of personal relationships, let's talk about IBM.

IBM 15 Minute Chart, Boobs, and Bananas

Once I had a job for about 3 months. I was the chief market strategist at a financial firm. It was a good job. I loved the people. But there was this one girl who would ask her boyfriend to take pictures of her at night (yes, those kinds of pictures), and then the next day she would send me an email with those photos attached. Some of you think that sounds like the perfect on-the-job situation. I hated it. I was trying to launch a currency-trading portal Web site, and she was sending me pictures of her boobies. Ugh.

Anyway, one day, she sent me a particularly explicit photo and I decided it was time to leave for the day before she started walking over and hovering around my desk. So I shoved my laptop into my bag, raced out of the office, and went to the movies. I think I saw "Burn After Reading," but I'm not sure.

I didn't take my laptop out of my bag for two more days. During that time, the computer was resting on top of an old banana. In that dark, cool space, the banana went soft. Over the next 48 hours, the banana actually got shoved into the air-vent holes in the laptop. The next time I turned on the computer, I didn't notice it because all the smooshy banana was underneath the machine. 20 minutes later, the entire house smelled like Banana Fosters. I was like, "Whoa, what is that delightful aroma? Who's cooking dessert?"

I mention all of this because that laptop was an IBM ThinkPad, and it ran like a champion, even with a banana inside. That cooked banana started to burn, and three weeks later the entire computer exploded. And guess what?

I called up IBM in the middle of the night and confessed everything. Just two days later I had a completely repaired laptop on my front porch. That's why I'd like to now spend a few minutes talking about IBM.

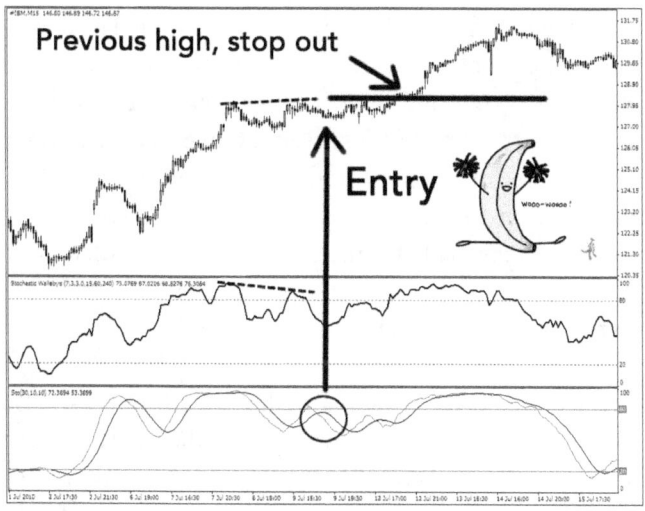

FIG. 8-15: IBM stops-out of a bearish divergence trade.

If you're wondering why I'm showing so many examples from the 15-minute charts, it's because I love that time-frame. I find that many of the successful trades I take are from this time-frame chart. Every trader is different, of course, and you might find that a different time-frame works better for you. But I like the 15-minute chart because the trades don't set up so frequently that I have to babysit the computer for 24 hours a day. And when the trades do fire off, I'm in the trades for about 1 or 2 days.

That seems to be the perfect amount of time for me.

This may actually be the best-looking trade setup in the entire book so far. Look at how both the Wallaby indicator and the regular Stochastic drop violently, even as the stock is making gradual higher highs. To see what I'm talking about, just look at the difference in the slope between the price of IBM and the Wallaby indicator. To me, that's when I start saying all those stupid things like, "This trade is a no-lose proposition," and I go out and buy a new car or television to pre-celebrate my impending success and election to the Hall of Fame of Great Trade-Predictors.

In reality, this trade stinks.

Because the stock made higher highs with price — also overbought – but made lower highs on the Wallaby, we've got bearish divergence. And that, my Friends, means we want to sell the crap out of the stock. We wait for an uptick, order some shares from our broker, place the trade, and wait for the sweet profits to start rolling in, Baby.

Wrong. What a crap trade!

At least it doesn't lose that much money, right? We have a stop-loss just above the highest point the stock reached before the trade entry. On a $127 stock, our stop-loss is at $129, just two bucks. Hardly anything at all, right? You can buy a pound of bananas for two bucks. Just a slight movement against us, and we give up on the trade.

As it turns out, we are rewarded (as usual) for making a quick exit. The stock travels about $4 higher still after we stop-out. No need to sit through that disaster. We're not trying to ride out the storm or prove how tough we are. A trader's toughness isn't measured by her ability to sit in a dumb trade for a long time. It's proven by her willingness to accept the loss and keep her composure long enough to take the next trade.

We've seen too many examples of stopping-out of sell trades. Let's toss out a bonus example and show what a buy trade looks like when it goes pear-shaped.

GBP/CHF 15 Minute

I get bored saying the same things over and over again. So, for this example, I'm going to show you a chart, and then I'm going to write a short play. The play will explain the chart. For those of you wishing to only read the sections of this book written in traditional, boring mass-market trading format, please skip the next few pages.

Behold, The Chart:

FIG. 8-16: GBP/CHF bullish divergence stop out.

Behold, The Play, Based Loosely on Henry Ibsen's *"A Doll's House"*:

A Dollar's House

ACT I

[SCENE – A well-appointed office trading area, with a 30-inch monitor and comfortable work chair. A bushy-mustached, handsome young man is inspecting a chart, back turned to audience. He is humming a tune, clearly in high spirits. At stage left, a small marsupial wearing a cowboy hat is lounging in a plush recliner, much too large for his frame, holding a remote control, flipping through channels.]

ROB: The pair is making lower lows! But on the Wallaby, it's making higher lows!

[Note to reader: see Figure 8-16].

WALLABY: Yeah. I noticed. I'm divergent.

ROB: I'm going to buy this currency pair. I can already feel that once I take this trade, it's going to save us from our financial problems.

WALLABY: I'm not the answer to your financial problems. But since you brought it up, where are you going to buy the currency pair?

ROB: When the regular Stochastic Oscillator makes a bullish crossover. Look, here. I've drawn an arrow on the chart to show where the entry will be.

WALLABY: *[clearly not paying attention]*. That's nice, Honey.

ROB: Fine. I can see you don't care. But this is going to be the big-time. I'm going to set a profit target for 100 pips. I'm feeling chills go up my spine.

WALLABY: Turn on the heat.

ROB: Very funny. You'll be excited for me, and you'll show me more love and attention when you see the trade profits roll in. Such pips you have never seen!

WALLABY: You are a hopeless dreamer. A reckless spender. That's all you'll ever be.

ACT II

[SCENE – Rob sits, pulling on hair while head in hands, back still turned. Wallaby now standing beside desk, hands on hips, head cocked to one side. Deep sighs heard from Rob.]

WALLABY: So, are these sweet profits here yet?

ROB: No. Nothing ever works for me.

WALLABY: You never dance with me. You were trading when we should have been dancing. Our relationship is falling apart. Yet you ignore me.

ROB: I'm a failure.

WALLABY: *[hands in pouch]*.

ROB: The GBP/CHF made fresh lows. I exited the trade where I drew this little circle. I couldn't stay in the trade any longer. I had already lost significant pippage. There shall be no Christmas presents in the Booker household.

WALLABY: I'm sorry to hear this.

ROB: What shall we do?

WALLABY: I'm considering committing suicide in order to cover up the terrible truth of your failed trade.

ROB: *[falling on Wallaby's breast, hand across forehead for effect]*. Please, no!

ACT III

[SCENE – Rob and Wallaby sit together in recliner, snuggly and lovey to each other. Wallaby uses paw/hoof/appendage to stroke Rob's hair in caring fashion.]

WALLABY: I forgive you.

ROB: Now I'm forever indebted to you. You have forgiven me and proven that you are my moral superior. With this act you have made me totally dependent upon you, as a child is to a parent. Or as a doll is to her child owner. Or a quote currency is to the base currency, or a foreign subsidiary to the multi-national corporation, or as George Bush was to Dick Cheney. Our relationship is premised on fanciful and unreasonable notions such as these.

WALLABY: ...Such as the ability of a marsupial and a human to mate?

ROB: No, that part has always been good. You know that.

WALLABY: How true that is.

ROB: You would never understand. You're just a narcissistic mammal with no capacity for empathy.

WALLABY: Shhh. I think "Top Chef" is coming on. The secret ingredient is kangaroo. I FRIGGIN' hate kangaroos.

[curtain].

Frequently Asked Questions About Wallaby Stops

There are three very common and important questions that I get about Wallaby stops.

What's the worst consecutive losing streak on Wallaby trades? My worst losing streak on the EUR/USD was three trades in a row. It happened during the period of time when the U.S. Federal Reserve was set to print one trillion dollars in the program called "Quantitative Easing." Just saying that almost sounds like a joke. But it's not. They really did that! This program of dollar-creation sent the EUR/USD flying out of control. As a note, the 1-minute chart (for any financial instrument) is prone to consecutive losses because a quick spike in price can take out our stop-loss. But because our risk:reward ratio is healthy, this generally is not a problem.

You might wonder what the worst losing streak will be for index futures, or stocks, or bonds, or something else that you're going to trade. I simply don't know a rock-solid answer to that. I don't trade those financial instruments every day. But I have watched every Wallaby trade on the 15- and 5-minute S&P charts for about a year now, and the maximum number of consecutive losses that I remember seeing was four. I suspect that's true of just about any security that you're going to trade with the system.

What about not using a stop? You're going to find that

you can get lucky every once in a while by staying in a trade and not stopping out. In the Figure 8-13 for Oil, it almost seems laughable to stop-out so quickly. Most traders would stay in that trade for much longer and let the contract rise $5 or more against them before they exited. While I'm sure that occasionally this works out just fine, I don't understand why we can't just take the loss, then set up the next trade. In every instance where I've taken the loss, and set up the next trade, I've been happy. Happier, indeed, than when I stayed in the losing trade and tried to "hope it back to break even."

Some traders have decided that instead of stopping-out of a Wallaby trade, they will simply wait for the next setup, and then double down on the entire move. This is called "Martingale" trading, and it's named after John Wilkes Booth, who shot Abraham Lincoln.

While that's not actually true, I do believe that staying in the trade and doubling down can be as dangerous as shooting the President of the United States. Just like an assassination attempt, it

a) seems like a good idea at the time;
b) is a way to release your anger;
c) it eventually turns out really crappy.

I find myself doing this very thing sometimes (doubling down — not shooting the President), and every time, and

I'm not making this up, I feel like chopping off my legs while I do this. Every single time, I kick myself. "Booker, what the hell are you doing?" I say to myself. Invariably, the second attempt at the trade turns out to be just as awful as the first (kind of like going back and dating someone you broke up with, even when you know she's no good for you). And then, with that second ugly trade, I'm in a far worse situation and wondering what to do about it.

It is a truth about trading that:

the greater the loss,
the less likely a trader is to accept it

The larger the loss, the more we want to avoid it, and the more willing we are to hold on and hope. I call this "Possum Trading," where you simply close your eyes and pray to St. Anthony that he will find your lost trades. We start doing crazy stuff when our trades go wrong. You promise God you'll stop looking at porn or yelling at your kids or eating chocolate-covered hamster paws by the cartonful at midnight. Even when God answers those prayers, you eventually do the same thing all over again, and then one day, He just gets really fired up and sends your favorite financial instrument off the charts, margin calls your account, and on top of that, he's damned you to hell. If you make a deal with the devil, you get a financial wedgie.

And then your partner makes you sleep on the couch for a year.

What about taking the loss on the first stop, and then doubling up on the next trade? The market let you down. You want your money back. Most people think that revenge trading is dangerous. I say it's unavoidable. If the market takes your money, you should go and knock it in the skull and get it back. One way to do this is to eat your crow, take your small loss on the first trade, and then, the second time around, when the trade sets up all over again — slightly increase the trade size and pound on the market. There are some of you shaking your heads right now in disagreement.

Booker, that's not a very responsible thing to do!

Oh, I know that. Like many of the things I do with my trading, it's not very traditional. It's also not what you hear from the average guru-type. But I employ this technique all the time when I stop-out on the first trade. However, I don't increase the size after the third trade. I just go back to trading the regular trade size.

Armed with the ability to minimize the negative impact of a failed trade, you're now ready to hear everything the Wallaby knows about taking profits. And this is where things get exciting.

9

Profit Targets for the Wallaby

There's no telling what you can do when you allow your mind to accept that abundance is the natural state of being. Before you can make any money trading, I say, you need to first understand that you deserve to be making money trading.

So many traders begin trading because something negative has happened in their lives. They've lost a job, run up their credit cards or find themselves in a precarious financial position, and they need a quick fix. The whole enterprise starts off from a negative perspective: I'm screwed, and I'm an idiot for getting into this situation, and now I gotta find a way out.

Not surprisingly, when we start off this way, our trading tends to reflect this very perspective. We start trading, and then we get ourselves into trouble, and then we get mad at ourselves, and then we desperately seek a way out of the trouble. Our cycle of trading follows the cycle of our lives. Have you ever felt yourself trapped in this pattern? I've been there.

If this cycle doesn't seem familiar to you, perhaps you started trading after a successful career or experience in some other arena. You come to trading with this mindset: I've been successful at running a corporation, so why wouldn't I be successful at trading?

People in this second category become really frustrated when profits don't come quickly. They expect success fast.

And trying to force profits to come quickly has a terrible effect on trading. You start to force trades. You start to increase the trade size (I'm smart; I'm powerful; I know what I'm doing). Many people in this category also feel uncomfortable sharing their results openly with others. They've been successful, and they don't see any reason to answer to other people. It's hard to ask for help when for years you've been in charge. Trading is made more difficult when you don't feel comfortable showing your weaknesses. Starting over from scratch is a humbling experience.

Why I Said All of That

From the start, before we conclude our discussion of the Wallaby trade with a bang, I want to encourage you to shift your perspective.

Rather than think of trading as a way out of a problem, or of another conquest, I want you to consider it a game. You're playing a game here, and no single round of this game is supposed to be very critical or important. The entire match is what matters. You're going to make some mistakes along the way. When you do, just move on and don't get attached to the result. When you have a good experience, a good trade, don't get attached to that, either. Play the match point that is now, and don't worry about what you just did, or what you think you need to do in order to pay the rent.

For this reason, I don't make weekly or monthly or yearly trading plans. And I sure as hell don't make any trading goals for anything except the trade in front of me. How am I going to know what I can plan for 6 months from now? At a maximum, I can know that a Wallaby trade is setting up right now, on the EUR/USD, and the only thing I can really do is plan to do my very best with this one opportunity. If I take care of business now, then the rest of it just takes care of itself.

Your ability to trade for a living is based on your ability to build profits over time, one trade at a time. Sounds obvious, but all of us can very quickly become obsessed with setting goals for what we're going to be able to buy with profits that we haven't made yet. And then, when things go wrong, we become obsessed with trying to get back the money we lost quickly.

Instead, just think about your next trade, or the trade you're in, and focus on getting that right.

I can't say it enough: Your only responsibility is to professionally manage your current opportunity.

Taking Profit with Support and Resistance

The easiest way to plan for a profit target on a Wallaby trade is to get out when you've seen your trade reach a previous high or low. You'll remember the basic concept of support and resistance from the chapter on stops.[1] If you want more help with the concept, I've included some helpful resources in the Appedix Three for you.

Exiting a Wallaby buy trade

Buy Profit Example 1: EUR/USD 15-minute

In Figure 9-1, the EUR/USD sets up a bullish Wallaby trade. Here's the chart:

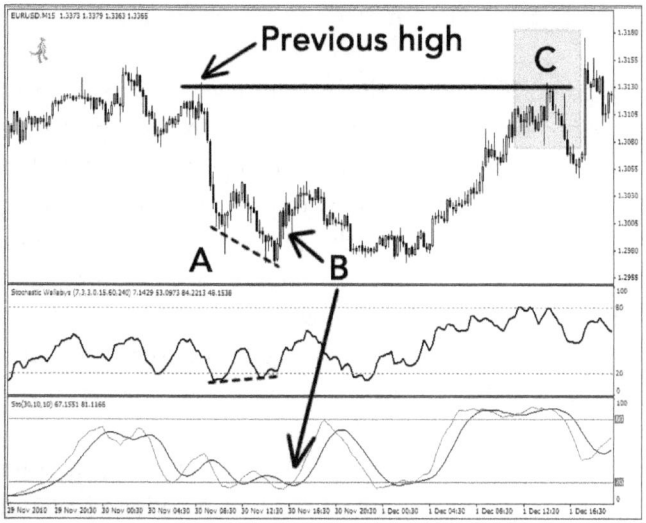

FIG. 9-1: Taking profit on a EUR/USD buy trade.

1. I miss that chapter. We had some good times back then, didn't we?

At point "A," the currency pair sets up a buy trade — it's bullish Wallaby divergence. The EUR/USD makes new lows, which are oversold, and at the same time the Wallaby makes higher lows. At point "B," we buy the currency pair because we see a bullish crossover on the regular Stochastic. The approximate price for entry is 1.3005.

You already know that our stop-loss will go below the lows that the pair made as it set up the trade — at about 1.2955, or a risk of 50 points (pips). This is not shown on the chart because it's the very bottom of the price scale (look at the far right edge of the chart).

At point "C," when the pair reaches its most recent previous high, we exit the trade. The price at that time is 1.3125 (I'm rounding down here), for a profit of 120 points. We risked 50 points to get 120. Nothing wrong with that. I'd love to keep that ratio going – with a risk of 1 for a potential profit of 2 – as often as possible. Sometimes the ratio is even better. Sometimes it's a bit worse. If the trade setup shows a risk of 1 point for a gain of 1 point, then I'll usually skip that trade and wait for the next one.

It's worth noting that there exist more complicated ways of planning a profit target. We'll even address some of those methods later on. But I want to say right now that this single example shows you everything that has ever been important to me on the subject of taking profit on a Wallaby trade. While it seems simplistic to just draw a line across a recent high and use that level as a profit target, I'm telling you that it doesn't get much better that this.

Buy Profit Example 2: HPQ 15-minute

In Figure 9-2, HPQ sets up a bullish Wallaby trade.

FIG. 9-2: HPQ sets up a bullish Wallaby trade.

Lower lows on price, higher lows on the Wallaby. That's all shown in point "A". Our entry at point "B" comes at around $39.30. You can already figure out that our stop-loss is going to go just below $39 – below the lowest point that the stock reached while it set up the Wallaby trade. For the sake of argument, let's say we put the stop-loss at $38.90, so if it falls to that level after we enter the trade, then we're getting out. That would be a loss of about 40 cents per share. Plus we have to pay transaction costs and the spread. Then we've got to tip the massage therapist to help us relax if we do in fact have an unhappy ending on the trade.

Our profit target comes at a previous high, and we don't even need to move to a different time-frame chart or look far back in time to find this level. In fact, the stock made a double top at about $40.50 just about a day ago (on the chart). That works just fine for a profit target. When the stock reaches that point ("C"), we can happily exit. It's a move of $1.30 per share, or 3% on the stock, which is a perfectly reasonable gain. And we risked only .40 to get it.

But wait. Is there more that we can do here?
Yes.
Am I going to tell you what that "more" is?
Yes.

Riding a Winning Buy Trade

I just love these trades because we can take a good profit target at point "C" and even make it better. If you're the type of trader that likes to ride your winners even longer, then the next chart is for you.

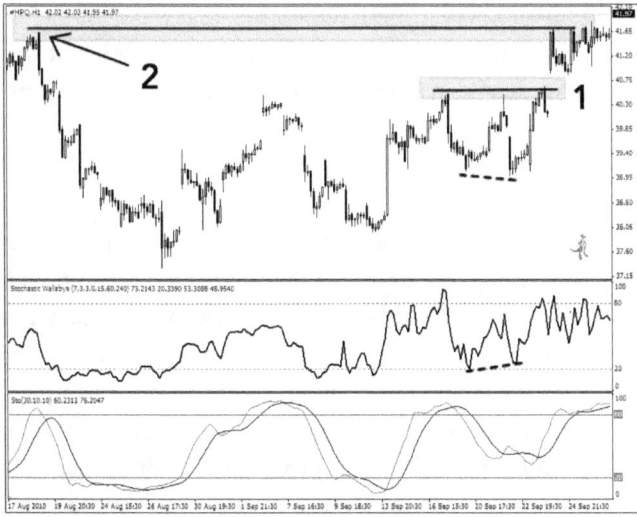

FIG. 9-3: Extending the profit target on HPQ.

For Figure 9-3, I've moved to the 1-hour chart. You can see the Wallaby divergence trendlines drawn on the stock on the right side of the chart, just to give you an idea of where we set up the trade in the first place. If you're having trouble finding those lines – just look for the dashed black trendlines on price and on the Wallaby.

I've moved to the 1-hour chart for the purpose of going back further in time, seeing more candles, so we can find a higher, previous peak on the stock — and we're going to use that as a secondary profit target for the trade.

A point "1" in the chart, we find our original profit target at about $40.50. As you'll remember, that was a 3% gain in the stock. But what if, instead of exiting the trade at that point, we stayed in longer? We can do that, and here's how:

1. **We stay in the trade.** When the stock reaches point "1," we don't exit the trade.

2. **Move our stop-loss.** Instead, we move our stop-loss to $39.30, so the worst thing that can happen now is that we end up with zero money lost on the trade. I've heard Jim Cramer refer to this situation as "playing with the House's money," and that's an accurate way to describe it. Some traders at this point sell part of their position and take some profit off the table. That's not my style, so I'm not even going to get into an expanded discussion of the topic. I say, if you believe the stock can go higher, stay in the entire position. If you don't think it can go higher, exit the entire position. Make a decision and stick with it.

3. **New profit target.** Now we have a new profit target at point "2," and as you know, we determined that level by looking back in time, as far back as necessary, and drew a horizontal line (a resistance level) at the last obvious peak. If you still don't understand how we found that peak or made that determination, please refer to the short Appendix Three resource section on support and resistance, or do some Googling of support and resistance, or buy a book, or just stop making it so difficult and just realize that we drew a line across a place where the stock previously couldn't go any higher.

What happens next? The stock moves up to the profit target at position "2," all the way at $41.60. That's a gain of $2.30 on the trade, or 5%. Could you move the profit target again, and move the stop again? And keep doing this forever?

The answer is yes. We'll talk more about this at the end of this chapter. For now, I want to make sure we talk about exiting a Wallaby sell trade.

Exiting a Wallaby sell trade

Sell Profit Example 1: Gold 30-minute

In next chart, you'll see that we enter a sell trade on Gold (spot price) at about $1,421. The precious metal has made higher highs with price (which are also overbought) and lower highs on the Wallaby. That's bearish Wallaby divergence.

Our stop goes above $1,431. Figure 9-4 shows two possible profit targets.

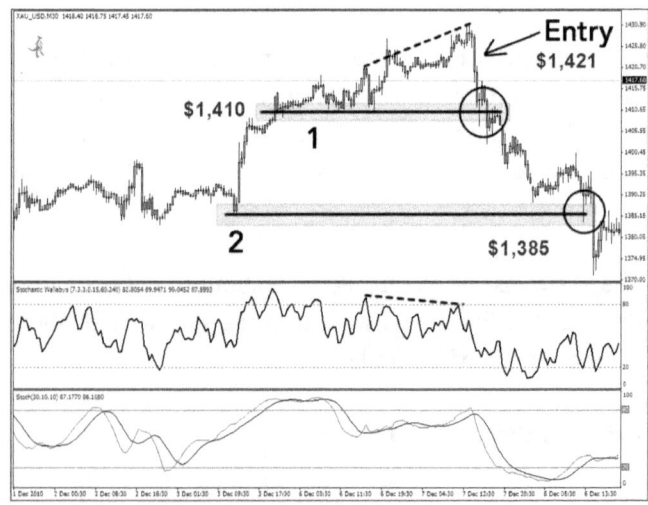

FIG. 9-4: Extending the profit target on Gold.

When Gold hits profit target #1, at approximately $1,410, we've made $10 on the trade (and you're most likely trading with leverage here, so the gain is multiplied by that leverage). It's an impressive gain already.

Here's where we have a choice. We can ring the cash register and close the trade. Or we can move the stop-loss on the trade to break even and see if God will send the sweet Cherubic Angels of Profit to serenade you. In other words, we're wondering if Gold can fall to profit target #2. In overnight trading, that's exactly what it does — it falls farther, all the way to $1,385 — which more than triples our trading profit to $35.

The precious metal falls even farther still afterward, but you get the idea.

Before we continue, I just want to remind you that this trade could have stopped out at a loss. We could have lost just over $10 on the trade (times leverage!). Not every trade will be a winner. By extending our profit target, we've given ourselves to make $35 on the trade in exchange for risking about $10. That's a very reasonable risk:reward ratio.

Sell Profit Example 2: USD/JPY 5-minute

Figure 9-5 shows bearish divergence. Our entry on the trade comes at 81.30.

The stop on the trade would come above the highs that the currency pair made before we took the entry. That number is about 81.67 (see the quotes at the far right side of the chart), for a maximum possible loss of 37 points.

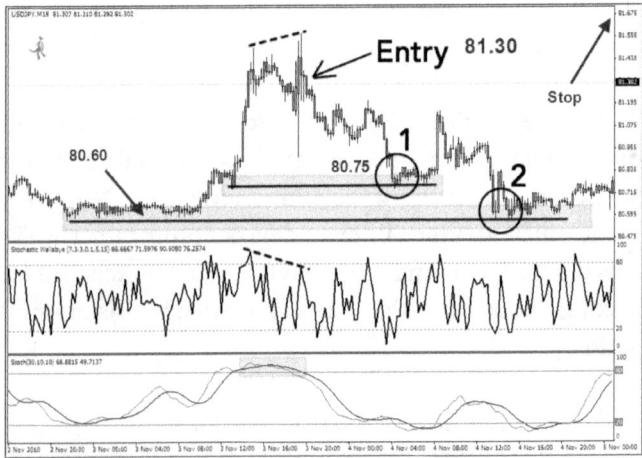

FIG. 9-5: USD/JPY trade. Profits 1 and 2 are near each other.

The currency pair makes higher highs on price, but lower highs on the Wallaby. You might also notice that the regular Stochastic Oscillator does not make separate overbought highs across the two peaks in price. Does that invalidate the trade setup? No. It's just a slightly perverted version of bearish Wallaby divergence, and we'll happily still take the trade. It's good to look at examples of trades that aren't quite perfect, right? Earlier in a previous chapter I mentioned that sometimes the best-looking trades end up performing terribly. And sometimes the trades that look bad end up with sweet, delicious profit. Just remember that!

Profit target "1" is at approximately 80.75. That's 55 points (pips) of profit, for an original risk of 37 points. Once again, our risk:reward ratio is just fine. But if we hold on for the second profit target at point "2," we can exit near the 81.60 mark, for a profit of 70 pips. Now we've almost gained twice as much as we risked on the trade.

Try it Yourself!

DIY Example 1: IBM 15-minute

Take a look at this 15-minute chart for the technology and consulting services giant, known for formerly producing laptop computers that could also make a delectable Bananas Foster. Chart:

FIG. 9-6: Look at Appendix Two for the answer.

What would you do here? Can you draw the divergence lines to set up the trade?

Take a moment and do the following:

1. **Set up the divergence trade.** Draw lines on the price, and on the Wallaby, and show me the divergence.
2. **Circle the trade entry.** Show me at which candle (approximately) we would enter the trade. Write your best estimate for the price at entry over that same area.
3. **Set the stop-loss.** Draw a border across the area where we'd stop out of the trade. If the stock moves past that line, the trade is over and we stop-out.
4. **Set the profit target.** Where is your first profit target? Does it reach that level? What did we risk on the trade compared to what we could have gained?

Now take a look at Appendix Two in the back of the book. See if you've drawn your lines and such in the same way I did. If yours are different but also somewhat similar, that's fine. But if you find that you took a trade in a completely different direction, or that this trade became a loss, then go back to the steps above, and try again, this time using the chart from the back of the book as a cheat sheet.

My Philosophy on Profit-Taking

The more comfortable you become at practicing with profit targets on historical charts, the more money you're going to make in live trading. For me, it's always easier to stay in a good trade than it is to exit it and then try to find a good place to re-enter. What I'm trying to say is, if you have a good thing going, you might want to consider stretching out the profitable run that you're having.

In this order, here are my preferences for dealing with a profitable trade:

1. **Move the stop and extend the profit target.** Every super-successful trader I know does this. Turn your winners into bigger winners. Increase the size of your average profit. Do this and you'll be able to ride out periods of time when the trades don't go as well. Do this and you'll learn to be patient.
2. **Exit the trade.** Just take the money and run.

As a reminder, I'm not a big fan of exiting part of the trade with a small profit and then letting the rest of the trade run. Again, here's my view: If you don't like the trade enough to stay in it, then get out.

If I've bought 100 shares of HPQ, and the stock has moved $1 in my favor, I've made $1,000. If I sell 50 shares and bank $500, that might be satisfying from a psychological perspective.

I'm left holding 50 shares. Was that a good choice?

Question: How far does HPQ have to move in order to net me the same profit — $1,000 — as I had when I was holding 100 shares?

Answer: It needs to move another $1 again. Just to get me the same profit I already had a moment ago!

If we'd just held onto all 100 shares, and the stock had moved another $1, we'd now have $2,000 in profits. If you think it can go up farther, let me ask you — why are you not holding onto the entire position?

"Because," you say, "I have no idea that it will go up, so I want to bank some profit now." And if you have no idea that it's going up, and you're unsure about staying in the trade, then why are you in it at all? Exit the whole position!

On the other hand, if you're confident that the stock can go up another full $1 (which is what it would take to at least equal the profit you already have), then just stay in the full position and move your stop so you won't take a loss. The very worst that can happen to you is that you end up with zero won, zero lost — minus some small transaction fees, of course. And then you wait for the next trade to set up, which doesn't really take that long (there are hundreds of these trades that set up every week across the universe of financial instruments).

By staying in the position longer when you have an obvious

next profit target, you help offset your transaction costs. You make more money for yourself. Remember, you have to pay taxes on these gains, and taxes can be substantial. You might as well do everything you can to make the most of what's going well.

And if you don't feel comfortable staying in the trade — just get out and take the money. Keep banking your gains.

What About Not Trying To Be a Hero?

Do you remember from a while back when I talked about not trying to be a hero? I want to make sure I clear up any possible confusion. It can sound like I'm contradicting myself when I say, "Don't be a hero," and then next thing you know, I'm saying, "Extend your profit target."

Most people will quickly close a winning trade. Even before it reaches the profit target they set at the very start (and they set that profit target based on experience and testing). They do this because they have lost so many times, and they're just very happy to finally have a good trade going. It's odd but true to say that many traders panic when they're winning — and they ignore the losses when they're holding onto bad trades.

You want to do the opposite. You want to panic when something's gone wrong. And by panic, I don't mean you should pee in your pants and start freaking out on your family. What I'm saying is that you should be quick to exit a bad trade.

So, back to the possible contradiction.

Being a hero is when you keep your winning trade open but do nothing to protect the profit. Trying to be a hero is when you say, "I know I could move my stop to break even, but I want to give the trade room to breathe." Hero-trading is when you want to act tough, instead of acting smart. Trying to be a hero is when you trade without a cutoff point for your bad trades, like a rock-climber without proper gear or a sailor without a life vest, or a hooker without a stash of condoms.

So, when I say that it's a good thing to extend your profit target, what I'm trying to communicate is that you try to make more money while simultaneously removing or reducing any possibility of loss.

How Do You Know When to Extend the Profit Target?

The honest answer is nobody knows. There are as many answers as there are traders. But here are two ways you can determine whether or not to extend your profit target. When the regular Stochastic is overbought or oversold. Let's use the example from Figure 9-5.

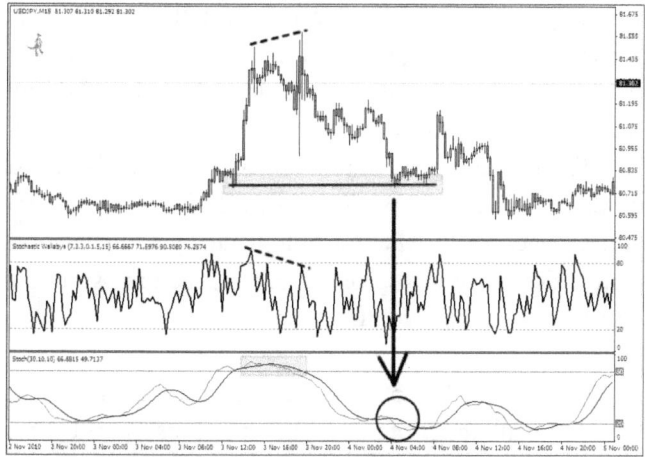

FIG. 9-7: When we hit profit target #1, we're OS.

In Figure 9-7, you can see that when we hit the first profit target on the currency pair, the regular Stochastic is already oversold (below the 20 line). That's one way that some people can decide to exit the trade and take the profits. However, I want to note that there are many, many examples of a financial instrument staying overbought or oversold for a longer period of time after it hits the 80 or 20 level. In fact, look back on your charts (and the examples in this book), and you'll find that there are plenty of times when the guideline I've just described will cost you money, instead of making you money.

So, with that said, here's Guideline #2.

Just flip a coin. Seriously, I gotta tell you straight: I have no frigging idea how to absolutely tell the difference between trades that go to profit target #2 (or 3, 4, 5 or 6 or 10) and the ones that stop at #1. Most of the time, I simply stay in the trade longer if I've made money for the week, and I'm just adding profit to an already successful string of trades. If I've lost money for the week, I stay in the trade longer, because — what the hell! It can't get much worse, and if I've made it to profit target #1, then my stop is at break-even, and I have a free ride.

If I'm just starting off the week of trading, I'm more likely to bank the profit at #1, because I just want to start making money and build up my confidence and get into the groove of trading. That's the way it works for me. It might seem arbitrary to you, but it's the way I do it. And I'd be happy to hear from you if you can test a better way to distinguish between the trades that go to #1 and the ones that go to #2.

I can't believe it, but we're already at the end of the book. Before I send you off to trade some Wallabies, I have a few last words for you.

APPENDIX ONE
SETTING UP YOUR CHARTS

Everything you read in this book can be applied to the stock market (including indexes and exchange-traded-funds – ETFs), futures, currencies, and bonds. I'm happy for you to apply it to any market you choose.

To display the Wallaby indicator on my charts, you're going to need two things: First, a charting program; Second, a Wallaby indicator or something equivalent.

When I say that you can use a "Wallaby Equivalent," I am saying explicitly that you don't need the Wallaby in order to trade the setups in this book. Other indicators work in similar ways, and that should work out just fine. When you look for an indicator that is similar to the Wallaby, you should look under the "oscillators" section of your charting program. That's where you'll find the indicators that measure overbought and oversold conditions.

Please remember that one indicator is not better than all other indicators. That kind of thinking gets traders into trouble, when they feel that they have discovered the Greatest Indicator Of All Time and they are going to pay off the U.S. deficit with their next trade. Finding the "best indicator" is not some universal search. I didn't create the Holy Grail of divergence indicators. I found something that works very well for me. But as you'll see on the Wallaby web site and blog – I'll post divergence charts using all sorts of different indicators, to show differences and similarities and so forth. The Wallaby is my primary tool for finding the divergence in the first place. But it's not the only way to do it, and it might not even be the best way for you.

Charting Programs

I've had the Wallaby indicator built for a variety of charting platforms, and it's available for free when you visit the Wallaby web site. As of the time of publication, the indicator was available for these platforms:

Metastock
Tradestation
NinjaTrader
FXTrek Intellicharts
Metatrader
eSignal
MotiveWave

And more are on the way. You can check on the Wallaby web site to see updates on new releases. If you want to have the Wallaby indicator on your charts, do two things: Call your broker and let them know to contact me, and also contact me and tell me to contact your broker.

The Wallaby Indicator or Something Equivalent

Let's say you're trading with a broker or charting platform that does not offer the Wallaby. No problem. Let's discuss some equivalents and how you can use them.

The Relative Strength Index (RSI)

Here's a chart with the Wallaby and the RSI (set to 13) plotted on the same SP chart.

FIG. A1-1: Wallaby and RSI together

As you can see from Figure A1-1, the Wallaby and the RSI look very similar. You can play around with your RSI settings to find something you like. I have found that the RSI can tend to find divergences that the Wallaby cannot, and also the other way around – the Wallaby sometimes finds divergences that the RSI does not.

The Commodity Channel Index (CCI)

Developed by Donald Lambert, the CCI measures how far an asset's price has deviated from its average. It's unique in the sense that it doesn't look – or move – in the same way as most other oscillators.

FIG. A1-2: The Wallaby and the CCI

In the above chart, the Wallaby and the CCI (set to 14) sit next to each other. They look and act quite similar: When the Wallaby moves up, the CCI tends to do the same. I've noticed that the CCI can make a sharper, more defined move than the Wallaby. So you'll see a lot of sharp angles on the CCI.

That's just two examples of oscillators that work as more than adequate substitutes for the Wallaby. If you find others – or invent your own – that work well for you, please let me know on the Twitter stream or on the Wallaby web site.

APPENDIX TWO
ANSWERS TO CHART QUESTIONS

Earlier in the book, I asked you to draw a set of lines on a chart, to test your knowledge of the Wallaby trade. This Appendix contains a chart, an answer, and an explanation.

If your notes and drawings on the charts are significantly different than mine, please don't launch any grenades or hurt anyone. Most of the time there will be slight differences in the way you and I think about these trades. However, now that I've said that – you need to know that if you get the trade direction incorrect, then you're messing up the entire concept of divergence and you should study the example more closely until you understand what you did wrong.

If, even after you study the example, you can't find out why you and I got a completely different direction on the trade, then make sure you're looking at the right example. If you still get a different answer, you might consider that you didn't make a mistake at all, but rather than the book contains an error. If that's the case, then I apologize profusely. That's unacceptable. I've double and triple checked these examples, so that shouldn't be the case. But if it is the case, I want you to know I understand how frustrating that is.

Answer to Figure 9-6

In Chapter 9, I asked you to identify some divergence on a chart. Here's my version of the chart:

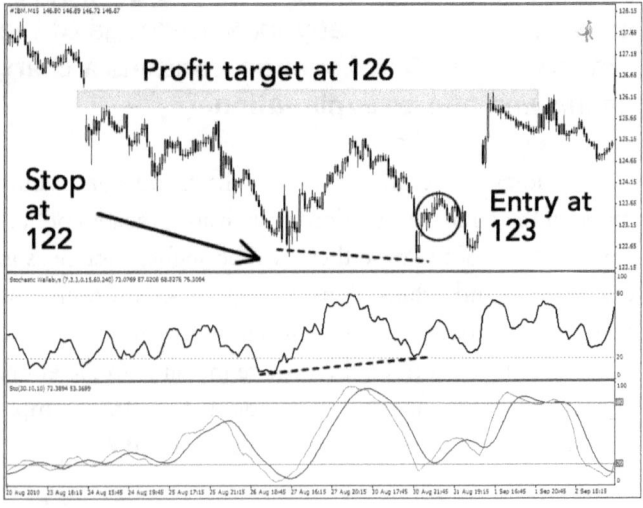

FIG. A2-1: Answer to Figure 9-6

I'm sure you found the bullish Wallaby divergence. The stock is making fresh lows on price while at the same time making higher lows on the Wallaby. Both areas are separately oversold on the regular Stochastic Oscillator.

Our buy entry comes at approximately $123, and the stop down below the lowest price the stock reached before it set up the trade. That's at about 122 (which is below the lowest quote displayed on the right side of the chart).

The profit target comes at about $126. That's a move of $3, or about 2% for the stock. A perfectly reasonable profit and risk:reward ratio.

There is no obvious profit target #2 on this trade. I'm sure if we moved to a higher time frame chart and went back further in time, we'd easily find a second profit target to work with here.

APPENDIX THREE
RESOURCES AND FURTHER READING

Support and Resistance

The best traders in the world understand the basic concepts of support and resistance. It doesn't matter if you're a trend trader or a counter-trend trader. It just makes sense to get a foundation in identifying these areas. There are two books that stand out, in my opinion:

"Pring on Price Patterns" (Martin Pring)

"Technical Analysis of Stock Trends" (Edwards and Magee)

Basics of Technical Analysis

Two books on this subject have been on my shelf for years. These are excellent introductions to the primary family of indicators and tools that traders use on their charts.

"Technical Analysis Explained" (Martin Pring)

"Technical Analysis of the Financial Markets" (John Murphy)

If you're going to spend a lot of time looking at the charts, it makes sense to have one (or both) of these references ready on your desk. I believe that trading systems come and go. There are lots of ways to make money trading. No one in particular has the single best method, or the one exact way that you have to use an indicator on a chart. That's why learning about the indicators for yourself can be so helpful. These two Web sites are also invaluable resources for diving into technical analysis:

investopedia.com
stockcharts.com/school

Economic Fundamentals

There are two references that I go back to time and time again:

"Currency Trading and Intermarket Analysis" (Ashraf Laidi)

"The Trader's Guide to Key Economic Indicators" (Richard Yamarone)

There are lots of other books on this subject, and Amazon is full of choices. I like Ashraf's book because it helps put pieces of the puzzle together and answer questions about how different financial instruments affect one another. The second book is valuable if you want to start to understand the usefulness (or uselessness) of economic numbers released by the government.

What it takes to be a trader

There is no one way to trade. Successful traders do not all look alike. They trade different markets, keep different schedules, favor the trend or trade against it, and so forth. Every successful trader finds her own way to the goal of trading for a living. I regularly refer back to these three books to remind myself that being a successful trader requires constant defense of one's individualism.

"Millionaire Traders" (Kathy Lien and Boris Schlossberg)

"Market Wizards" (Jack Schwager)

"Reminiscences of a Stock Operator" (Edwin Lefevre)

More Books

Although I have a large and growing collection of trading books, I find that books on other subjects are far more important. I believe that traders don't read enough poetry, history or fiction. Seriously! I'm not joking around.

The vast majority of traders want to spend all their time thinking about the markets. When it comes to being a patient, independent-thinking, cut-your-losses, ride-your-winners type of trader, however, there isn't anything better than reflecting on other subjects.

A few books come to mind, although this list is far from exhaustive.

"Good to Great" by Jim Collins may be the best trading-as-a-business book ever written, and it's not even about trading. It's about running a great company for the long haul. The lessons from great companies contained in the book are 100% applicable to becoming a great trader. His companion book, *"How the Mighty Fall,"* is equally stunning in the clarity with which he describes how businesses and (as you'll see) traders fail.

Speaking of failure, I highly recommend Jared Diamond's excellent work, *"Collapse,"* for the same reason. Study the grand failures in world history, and you'll start to see a pattern of self-sabotage that emerges in individuals and societies. Avoid these pitfalls, and you just might stay solvent long enough to trade for a living.

Most people hate poetry, and I'm not going to lie — it's not my favorite. But when I take the time to sit down with something by Walt Whitman, or John Milton, or Dante, or Robert Frost, my mind changes gears. Parts of my brain wake up. I see the world a little bit differently. For goodness sakes, get out of your element! Read something that stimulates your brain hopper!

Good fiction plays the same role. My favorite work of fiction might be Joseph Conrad's *"Heart of Darkness."* You think you're not prone to temptation? You think you're going to do something your own way, ignore the warning signs in front of you, and everything will be okay? So did Kurtz. And the next thing you know, the guy's eating human flesh and running around naked in the jungle.

Last of all, biographies of successful people are my favorite way of reminding myself of the basic ingredients to a successful endeavor: persistence, frugality, fiery determination and luck. Of every book you could choose in this category, there is one that stands out apart from the rest. It's Ron Chernow's *"Titan,"* which chronicles the life of the greatest American businessman who ever lived — John D. Rockefeller. Do not pass up the chance to digest the book and the lessons from the life of America's richest man.

In short, please read more, and read more expansively. And listen to, watch and involve yourself in activities that are positive. Fill your life with positive people. Delete from your life people and situations that are toxic. Does someone think you can't trade for a living? Shut them up or turn them off by never talking to them again.

APPENDIX FOUR
TESTING THE WALLABY

Some people will read this book (I'd guess three to four people, at least) and then immediately begin to trade the Wallaby. There's no substitute for learning how to trade a system using real money. There's also no better way to needlessly lose money. It's a trade-off: While it's true that paper trading doesn't give you the same adrenaline rush as live trading — and therefore, it's not as "accurate," in a sense — it's also true that paper trading simply helps you get the foundation down before you commit to anything.

There are two kinds of paper trading or "testing," as I call it.

The first style of testing involves moving backward in time on your charts, and then playing the candles forward and identifying every trade setup that emerges. Then you watch the trade setup play out and test your theories about how price should move. You can do this by programming rules into software and having it spit out a report. You can do this manually by scrolling back on your charts or by using a program such as Forex Tester (which simplifies this entire process for currency trading). Because this style of testing lets you move through a substantial amount of market activity in a relatively short period of time, I'd recommend working through at least 200 to 300 setups before ever trading with real money. It sounds like a lot of testing, but it's an enjoyable process.

If you're a short-term trader — a day-trader — then I'd strongly recommend spending 15 to 20 minutes every day before your trading session running through 10 to 20 trades in the manner described above. It sets the tone for the trading day, and it sets your focus.

Once you've completed this process, it's a good idea to move on to the second style of paper trading. This involves opening a demo account (or a practice account) with your broker — or tracking a virtual portfolio online. You can do this easily for futures, stocks, and forex, and there really isn't any excuse for not getting yourself set up to do this. When you have your virtual portfolio or demo account open, you simply watch for and trade real setups that occur in live market conditions, but you commit only "practice" dollars to the trades. I'd recommend opening the practice account with the same amount of money you intend to trade when you open the account with real money. I'd also suggest that you work through at least 20 to 30 trades with a system in this manner before you trade live.

A very small percentage of people, less than 1%, I'd imagine, ever do either of these kinds of testing before they trade. I'd suggest you become part of the 1%. When you test before you trade, you accomplish the following:

You understand the rules of the system. You don't want to be wondering about what to do in the heat of the moment when a trade is going wrong. We make terrible decisions as traders in these tense moments. Our monkey-lizard brain takes over, and we invariably revert to fight-or-flight mentality and end up either fighting the market (bad idea) or fleeing a perfectly good trade because we freaked out (also a bad idea). You don't have to go all fight-or-flight on your trading account! There's a third way, and it's called Sticking With the Plan. Most traders don't even have a plan to start with, so they're obviously going to be making all kinds of crap up on the fly, while in the worst possible emotional state. You don't want to be part of that crowd.

You'll take the trades you plan. When you test for a significant length of time before you trade, you're likely to take every trade your system produces. Have you ever found that you can talk yourself out of a perfectly good trade for reasons that don't have any bearing on the system you're trading? I find that when I'm reading Twitter updates from people I respect, I start to wonder if they know more than I do, and if I shouldn't avoid my next trade on the EUR/USD. We all do this. No one is immune. If you think you are, then you're God, and I'll see you on Sunday.

You won't take the trades you don't plan. Another terrible thing I've done in the past is take off-plan trades. You know what those are. They're trades you never planned to take but suddenly seemed like a good idea. They rarely are. You see a recommendation from someone, and you blindly follow it. Then you find out later they really didn't take the trade you thought they did, or something to that effect. It's a terrible habit. It's impulsive. We all fall prey to this once or twice (or many more times, in my case) in our trading careers. When you test before you trade, you're less likely to follow someone else's advice, and you're more likely to follow your own plan. Because you put time into it, it means more to you. Because you've invested substantial effort into your trading success, you're less likely to want to invest your resources on someone else's idea.

I have already said it, but it's worth repeating: Testing is the engine that drives the profit machine. Trading isn't easy. Trading is perhaps the hardest profession that you can choose. Testing doesn't ensure success, but it can help you avoid common problems. While it's true that past performance is not indicative of future results — which means that even a system that tests profitably in the past is not a guarantee of success — it sure as hell beats not having any idea what you're going to do every day.

For more information about the testing that I've done on the Wallaby — and more than 200 charts of the EUR/USD — visit the WallabyTrade.com Web site, and look for the keyword "testing."

APPENDIX FIVE
DEALING WITH ADVERSITY

Not all trades (or people, for that matter) can be winners. I spent all my high school years wandering around the halls, hoping the bell would ring and save me from looking stupid and alone. I, just like anyone else, struggle with self-doubt and times when I feel like giving up. The absence of adversity isn't a sign of success; it's a sign that you're not trying to do anything worthwhile.

It's only human to wonder if you should quit trading a system (or at all) when you have a few losses in a row. How many losses in a row are too many?

For Wallaby trades, you really shouldn't ever see more than four consecutive losses. With about 1% lost per trade (if you handle your money management well), that's not a big deal. I'd be all right with even six or seven losses in a row. I wouldn't start to get worried about it until after that point. If I have consecutive losses, I have to consider why I took those losses before I get overly concerned.

First, I ask myself: Did I follow the rules when I took these trades? If the answer is yes, then I'm fully ready to have six or seven losses in a row, if that's what happens. And I'm not going to worry about it. Because I followed the rules, I should be okay. If I didn't follow the rules — if I took early entries or dumb exits, then I need to stop trading for a day or so.

Second, I ask: Did I take larger than usual (more than 1%) losses on these trades? If the answer is yes, then I need to stop trading — for at least a week. If you find yourself taking big losses, then the problem is not with the system. The problem is that you're gambling, and you need to stop. In a moment I'll mention some things you can do when you stop trading for a time.

What if you have a losing month? For those of you who are planning on trading for a living, the question arises: What happens if you go an entire month, and you've lost money? My answer is: You take your living expenses out of your account, and you move on to the next month. And you've had a net withdrawal on the account. Not what you'd want, but that's life. Not every month is going to be a winner.

If you're thinking that traders like Steve Cohen (of SAC fame — it's one of the largest hedge funds in the world) don't ever have losing months, you're missing the point. Individual traders at his firm do in fact have losing months. Every honest trader on the planet is going to have losing months. It's just going to happen. When it does, you just move forward. Don't change too much, unless you've been breaking all kinds of rules with your trading. And if you're breaking all kinds of rules with your trading, then you deserve to have a losing month.

As I was writing this book, I started breaking rules and holding onto losing Wallaby trades — and I'm the author of this book! What a jackass, right? Well, we're all that same jackass sometimes. We all do this. None of us is exempt from making mistakes.

The best traders in the world go through periods of time when they're self-destructive. There's not one exception to this — not Warren Buffett (see his investment in Solomon Brothers), not Steve Cohen, Julian Roberston, Stan Druckenmiller, or any of the "market wizards" you've read about. Every great trader has a story about the time he was a complete screw-up. Coming back from that is part of what makes you, one day, a great trader.

In other words, the definition of being a great trader isn't the absence of mistakes; it's the ability to deal with mistakes in a positive manner and come back.

To prepare yourself for a losing month, I'd recommend setting aside profits each month or week — a rainy day fund, in other words — to compensate for times when the market doesn't cooperate, for those times when you've followed the rules and you got smacked around. Then, when you have a month that just doesn't work out, you can take a bit out of your rainy day fund, and you might not have to withdraw money from your trading account.

Another idea is to set aside one extra month (or two) of living expenses before you even start trading, so you're mentally prepared for that one bad month. Maybe it will never happen. By preparing in advance for it, the prospect of having a bad month won't scare you (and you're likely to do much better if you aren't afraid). One of the smartest things a trader can do is lower her living expenses. Everything in life is easier when you don't have money problems. I have found that there are very few problems in life that cannot be solved with cash.[1]

If you have a losing month (I know I'm repeating myself here), and it's because you didn't follow your rules, then you're in trouble. It means that you took what should have been a good month and you turned it into a bad one. What's to say you will ever have a winning month again? Not much. If you can't follow your trading rules, then stop trading, and go do something else that doesn't require following rules, like running for Congress or being president of a small, Caribbean nation.

Make a decision to make it work. I decided some time ago that I wasn't going to let adversity get in the way of something I want to do. One reason I don't set goals is that I believe goals are things you want to do, things you're going to try to accomplish. Here's how I view it: You either get stuff done or you don't. I don't set goals. I just decide to do things — or not to do things. And it's as simple as that. Once I decide to do something, that's the end of the discussion. I just do it.

When you're faced with adversity in trading, it's easy to suddenly find yourself re-evaluating whether or not you should continue. I think that's a load of crap. Whether or not you're going to trade for a living is a decision you make one time. At some point in time you still have a trading account, and you're trading for a living, or you don't have a trading account anymore, and you're not. If you're constantly trying to make up your mind about something, you're losing valuable time in actually getting that something done.

I'm not saying you should keep depositing money in your trading account (also known as flushing your life's savings down the toilet). But I am saying that you set a certain amount of money aside, and then you —

Protect that money
Trade that money

If you focus well enough on #1 above, then #2 takes care of itself. Seriously! I'm not joking around here. If you protect the base account balance, then you're going to find yourself in a position to make money over time, even with a losing month — even with two losing months!

---

1. Relationship problems cannot be solved with cash. But therapy might help, and guess what therapists like to be paid with? Cash! Other problems that you can solve with cash: loneliness, tooth decay, hunger, boredom, lack of style, and of course, poverty.

When to stop: I'll repeat a few reasons that you should stop trading. If any of these things happen, then stop.

You aren't following your rules, and you've lost more than 5% of your account balance.
You lose more than 10% of your account balance in any period of time.
You regularly take trades that you did not plan to take (whether profitable or not).
You regularly do not take trades that you did plan to take. (This comes from second-guessing too much.)

When these things happen, and you stop trading, there's a three-step process I'd encourage you to follow:

Transparency. Talk to your spouse or parent about what you've done. Get it out in the open and hide nothing. Bring account statements and journal entries to the conversation. Transparency solves nearly all trading problems.

Testing. Return to testing your system. Follow the steps I've outlined for testing, and do a crap-ton of additional testing for the system you trade. By re-testing what you already (should) know, you reinforce the good stuff. You remember how to avoid the bad stuff.

Time. Never be afraid to take time off from trading. Take a day off now and then, after a loss or a big win. Take a week off on a regular basis. Make this time off a total vacation from the markets. Clear your head. Get away from the computer. When you feel yourself sort of losing your trading balance, then step off the carnival ride and take a break. Traders often ask me, "But what if this means I'm going to miss some of the best trades?" I just answer, "There will be 1,000 Wallaby trades between now and the end of the year. Are you thinking that the very most important one is coming today?" One trade should never matter. Stop worrying about missing out on trades, and start worrying about missing out on life.

This advice wasn't comprehensive. There's room in an entire book to talk more about dealing with losses and wins, but this should get you started.

APPENDIX SIX
WHAT TO TRADE

What financial instruments work well with the Wallaby? Here are some thoughts.

First, trade the securities you know. If you know stocks, then I'd suggest sticking with stocks. Don't alter your trading plan to trade some new financial instrument because you heard that it works better. If you're familiar with the essentials of trading stocks, then it makes sense to first apply what you've learned in this book to something you already know. However, if you feel that you've got to make a change, and you want to start trading something different, pick up a book and start reading on the Web about the new financial instrument you've chosen. Spend a couple of months getting familiar with the new market before you make any moves.

Second, trade the time frame you know. If you're a day trader, then it doesn't make sense to pick up a book and expect that overnight you're going to become a long-term trader. As you already know, day traders and long-term traders have different mentalities, varying degrees of patience with trades, and so forth. If you have decided that now is the right time to make a switch on which time frame you want to trade, I'd suggest picking up a good book on trading psychology, such as Mark Douglas's excellent tome, "Trading in the Zone," or visit Brett Steenbarger's insightful blog (just Google his name; he's famous) and start reading.

You've already figured out that the key here is patience. There's no magic financial instrument or time frame. What matters is that you take the necessary time to get familiar with who you are, with what you're trading, and your expectations for the time frame in which a trade will complete. That's what matters.

With all of that cleared up, I'd like to talk a bit about four markets: stocks, stock indexes, futures and currencies.

Stocks. If you're going to trade the Wallaby on stocks, I've looked at some of the bigger names — IBM, HP, XOM — and I liked what I saw. Even on the shorter time frame charts, I liked the way these stocks moved with the divergence setups. If you have experience and trade other stocks (including smaller cap issues), I'd love to hear from you about your experiences with the Wallaby.

Stock Indexes. You can trade the indexes through futures contracts, ETFs, options, mutual funds — a variety of ways. I want to clearly state that before you trade any stock index with the Wallaby, you should put your testing time in. I'd suggest at least 500 tested trades and at least 50 live paper trade setups before you commit real money. Successful stock index traders are some of the smartest, most dedicated, most tenacious people I know. And you'll be trading with them when you choose to trade the $SPY or the $ES. The Wallaby can work fine with these financial instruments, but you're definitely running with the big dogs when you join this crowd.

Futures. Corn, beans, oil — you name it. Futures trading has lost some volume to currencies over the past 10 years, but it's still a huge business with tens of thousands of traders specializing in these issues. Futures trading is exchange-driven, which means that there's a certain amount of price transparency, which is very appealing to some. Also, you can easily access depth-of-market information, which for some is very important. I don't trade futures at all. It's not my thing. But I've been watching the Wallaby on a variety of futures contracts — in particular, oil — for some time now, and I like what I see. If you're a futures trader and you have an interest in testing and trading the Wallaby, I'd love to hear more from you.

Currencies. I trade currencies exclusively, and my primary vehicle for Wallaby trades is the EUR/USD. I also very much like the way the Wallaby sets up trades on the USD/JPY on the shorter term (5- and 15-minute) charts. The currency market has enormous liquidity. It moves very fast. It offers substantial leverage, even after government regulations in 2010 forced margin requirements upward. If you enjoy macroeconomics, trends that last for long periods of time, and a fast-moving market, then currencies might be a good fit. However, I'd suspect that more than 95% of currency traders lose money on a regular basis. Because the market moves fast, and especially because so much leverage is offered, it's easy to lose a substantial amount of money very quickly. If you choose this market, I strongly caution you against diving in without completing your testing first.

I'm always interested in hearing from you if you trade the Wallaby on any financial instrument, any time frame, in any market.

APPENDIX SEVEN
MONEY MANAGEMENT

When I look back on this book, I think I should have written 150 pages about risk and five pages about the Wallaby. I'm sorry I didn't do that.

When we start out as traders, we rarely consider the risks. We start off thinking about the rewards. It's natural. Wealth is a motivating force. We are attracted to what we want, and we focus our minds on it. The thought that we might someday accomplish something great (a profitable trade, a series of profitable trades or trading for a living) drives us forward, even during the bad times. However, the hope of making a lot of money can also be a disastrous emotion, pushing us onward, even when we have proven that we are impulsive risk-takers.

It's important to know yourself before you start trading. And it's important to understand what this book is about, and what it's not about. To a certain extent, after I write this book and you have it in your hands, it's your book, too. I did the best job I could writing it. And you clearly want to do the best job possible implementing what you've learned. What you do from here on out is up to you. I can't push the buttons for you. I can't place your trades for you.

At the same time, I want to repeat something I said many times earlier in this book: Please consider keeping a tight stop on your Wallaby trades. A stop just above the highs or just below the recent lows would be fine. These trades aren't deserving of your patience or hope. Hope is not a trading strategy. If the trading isn't working out, it isn't working out. You just move on and get out. If you've broken this rule, and you've let a trade go against you, it becomes harder and harder to close as it gets worse. It's a terrible reality about trading.

If you set a stop-loss at the time you enter your trade, it's done. If you set a reasonable small trade size on each trade to begin with, you've done more than most traders do. If you never overextend yourself, it's hard to imagine getting into terrible amounts of trouble on these trades. Step one is to simply limit the risk you take on each individual trade. Trading for a living isn't about scoring the big win, no matter what you read in the headlines about famous traders hitting the jackpot. For every giant trade that led to an enormous payoff for a famous trader like John Paulson, there are at least 100 individuals or funds that went bankrupt. It's why you hear about just a few people making huge money in the financial crises, but you hear about thousands of people who were wiped out. As traders we fixate our minds on the big winners, and we associate ourselves with them, forgetting how easy it is to become just another losing statistic. Please don't do that.

The second most important thing you can do is to ride out your winners. I know I've said this repeatedly. I know I've not been the best example of this in my own trading. I'm better at writing these words than I am at following through on them. But the fact is that most of us stay in our losing trades longer than we should, and we don't stay in our winning trades long enough. Turn it around. Our fearful trading mind — the mind that remembers the losses — is so happy to have a win that we quickly move to bank the profit before a trade is fully mature. Our hopeful mind looks at a loss and dreams that it can (and should) turn around. In each case, we are met with disappointment. I've found that even traders with very modest profit targets on their trades tend to close the trades out early. It doesn't seem matter if we're going for 10 points or 100. When the trade starts moving to our profit target, we become protective of it. It's like we're still living in caves and protecting the kill we made, because we know it could be weeks before we find another antelope out on the plains.

If you're having trouble with this (and most of us do at one point or another), here are some thoughts that have helped me.

If you find that you just can't get into the habit of letting your winning trades ride all the way to the profit target, start with just one or two trades. It doesn't matter which trades they are. After you've taken a few modest profitable trades for the week, consider letting the next two trades ride out longer, all the way to your profit target. Don't try to make a lot of progress in a short time. Just do it once, with one trade. One step forward is better than no step at all. Don't try to pick the "best" trade. Just pick a trade, from the start, and decide that this one trade is going to stay open longer if it is profitable. Then do it again another time. Don't put yourself on some kind of schedule or deadline to do this. Just do it when you can, and the habit starts to form. Most of us never become great at this; I've met thousands of traders, but very few are consistently able to stay in their winning trades all the way to the profit target.

I hope this is just the beginning of our conversation about risk management. For me risk control is more about psychology than it is about numbers. Let me know what you discover for yourself.[1]

---

1. For more information about the numbers side of risk management, I recommend Ralph Vince's heavy-on-the-math "Handbook of Portfolio Mathematics," which I've not been able to completely digest all the way myself, but it has been equally challenging and thought-provoking.

APPENDIX EIGHT
THOUGHTS ON COUNTER-TREND TRADING

What's the definition of a trend? Is it a move on the daily chart with higher highs and higher lows? Is a trend only a trend when a financial instrument stays above its 20-period weekly moving average? When does a correction become a full-blown trend?

These are reasonable questions in a book about counter-trend trading. In many examples of trades in this book, I've shown a 15-minute time-frame chart, with a counter-trend divergence trade setup. But that trade could very possibly coordinate with an overall trend on a longer time-frame chart. When you look at it from that perspective, you're trading with the trend, rather than against it.

FIG. A8-1: An upward trend on the 1-minute EUR/USD.

If you took a counter-trend trade on the EUR/USD, using Figure A8-1 as your chart, you'd be selling the pair. But if you did that, you'd be trading in the direction of the overall, 4-hour trend from the chart in Figure A8-2. So which is it? Is it a counter-trend trade or a trend trade?

FIG. A8-2: A downward trend on the 4-hour EUR/USD.

It doesn't really matter what you call it. That's what I say. This is a book about trading against the recent trending movement on whatever time-frame chart you're looking at. In that sense, this is a book about counter-trend trading. It is always going to be the case that you're trading with someone else's trend, and against someone's else's trend. And there are always going to be naysayers. It won't matter which direction you trade. If you start talking about your trades in public, you'll always find someone who thinks you're an idiot. After a while, we all learn to follow what we have tested and stick to our own plan, or we don't. It's not very complicated.

People sometimes wonder if it's reasonable (or responsible) to try and "pick a top" on a short-term chart.

He who tries to pick a bottom only gets a stinky finger.
— Rob Booker

About once a week when I take a trade, someone on Twitter mentions how ridiculous it is that I've tried to pick a top or a bottom. And my answer is this: Every single time you're taking a trade, you're making a choice about the direction of a financial instrument. You're either betting that it will continue to go up or down, or that it won't. Saying that one style of trading is smarter, safer, more responsible, wins more of the time — or whatever, is preposterous. Do you want to know what works best? Finding what works for you, and shutting out the rest of the chatter. Cutting off your losses quickly so when things go wrong, you don't suffer a loss of a substantial amount of your account. Riding out your winning trades. Those are timeless principles, and they don't have anything at all to do with trends or counter-trends.

APPENDIX NINE
AN INVITATION

I hope you'll do the following:

Follow me on Twitter. You can find me at @robbiebooker on Twitter, and from there I'll get you on your way to following Wallaby trades (which by the time of publication also has its own Twitter account). Here you'll see me post Wallaby charts, talk about the market generally, and do some wise-cracking. This is a great place to ask questions, post your own charts and engage in conversation.

Mark up the book, do some testing, stay in touch. Write questions and comments in the margins of this book. Scan the page where you have questions and upload it to Twitter and ask me about it. Do some testing and post the results. Engage in conversation with other traders about this — or about anything. Just get out there and start communicating with other people. We generally do better when we openly talk about our trading.

Post your trading results. Use a service like Profit.ly or just blog it. Post your trade results. There isn't anything better than accountability. It's the best form of motivation and discipline that I know. Let the world see what you're doing. Don't worry about people copying you. You're not engaging in arbitrage on wheat futures across three world markets. You're just taking a trade. If you buy IBM, you want everyone in the world to know it, and to buy it with you, right?

Ask questions. Some ideas for questions:

What indicator works best for me to set up divergence trades?

It's not necessarily the Wallaby Indicator. You might find that the CCI or the Momentum indicator work better for you. I welcome variety and individualism in trading. At the heart, this is a simple book about trading against the recent trend. And there are hundreds of ways to do it.

Consider looking at candle patterns or price patterns when planning divergence trades. Consider comparing the way that you do it with the way that other traders do it. If this book is a starting point for you to consider this type of trading, I will have done what I wanted to do.

I'm not the starring actor in your trading life. You are. The Wallaby isn't important. It's not the only or best indicator. You're the most important element in your trading. Let your creativity out. If you would like to suggest improvements, tell a story about how you altered an indicator to plan divergence trades — I'd love to hear from you. Please stay in touch about that.

Can I trade with the trend better than against it?

In the previous appendix, we tackled this question. There is no one trend or one counter-trend. There are movements on all kinds of charts, and they don't always say the same thing. However, if you find a trend on a daily chart, can you find good places to trade with that trend by using the Wallaby Trade on a shorter-time frame? Can it help with your entries? Do you find that these kind of "trend trade Wallaby Trades" work better for you in testing?

What is the optimal amount of risk per trade for me?

Are you taking too much risk in your trading? How much risk is appropriate for you? I strongly encourage you to deeply think about this by yourself and with a group of traders. Think about this question in mathematical terms, and in psychological terms.

From a mathematical standpoint, think about how often you win versus how often you lose. Think about the size of your average win against the size of your average loss. Think about the number of consecutive losses that you've experienced in your testing and live trading. Think about the size of the biggest loss you experienced in testing: What percentage of your total account balance was it? What percentage of your net profit over the preceding 20 to 30 trades was it? There are hundreds of additional ways to think about risk, and it bears repeating: When you get a handle on risk, you get a handle on your trading. It's not about magical indicators. It's about not losing money … and then making money.

When you think about risk from a psychological perspective, consider how you feel when you are in a losing trade. What are your tendencies in that situation? How well do you handle losses? Gains? Do you become wild and angry when you lose? Or euphoric when you win? How does that affect your trading? Is one type of emotional state more beneficial to your trading? Can you trace your emotions on each trade and find how those emotions have played a role in your performance? How do your relationships affect your trading? I could keep listing out questions like this all day long, but you get the point.

What do I want to get out of trading?

Start with the end in mind, as Stephen Covey would say. Are you trying to make enough money to pay your mortgage? All your living expenses? What is success in your mind, when it comes to monthly trading performance? Is it about never having a losing month (which is probably impossible). Is it about never having a losing day (which is definitely impossible). What exactly do you believe you're capable of doing, and what do believe the market is capable of providing to you?

What is my worst trading habit? What's my best?

Where do you fail most consistently? Is there something you can do about that? Who have you told? What is the consequence of not doing something about your worst trading habit right now? Where will you be as a trader in 12 months, if you do nothing about it? Will you still be trading in five years if your habit becomes worse?

What would happen if you amplified your best trading habit? What would occur? What if you became even more skilled at that one thing? Perhaps it is one particular kind of trade setup: You just seem to do it better than anything else. But you don't focus on it exclusively because it doesn't produce "enough" trade setups. That's bullocks! What would happen in five years if you totally focused on what you did best and you let everything else go?

 Try it.

ACKNOWLEDGEMENTS

Thank you:

To Roger Harmon for being my Wallaby trade friend from the beginning,

To Jason for editing this book,

To Wes for organizing my entire life,

To Joe for designing this book,

To Jennifer for inspiring me,

And thank you for reading.